The Community College and Its Critics

L. Steven Zwerling, *Editor*

NEW DIRECTIONS FOR COMMUNITY COLLEGES
ARTHUR M. COHEN, *Editor-in-Chief*
FLORENCE B. BRAWER, *Associate Editor*

Number 54, June 1986

Paperback sourcebooks in
The Jossey-Bass Higher Education Series

Jossey-Bass Inc., Publishers
San Francisco • London

EDUCATIONAL RESOURCES INFORMATION CENTER
ERIC — Clearinghouse For Junior Colleges
UNIVERSITY OF CALIFORNIA, LOS ANGELES

L. Steven Zwerling (Ed.).
The Community College and Its Critics.
New Directions for Community Colleges, no. 54.
Volume XIV, number 2.
San Francisco: Jossey-Bass, 1986.

New Directions for Community Colleges
Arthur M. Cohen, *Editor-in-Chief;* Florence B. Brawer, *Associate Editor*

New Directions for Community Colleges (publication number USPS 121-710) is published quarterly by Jossey-Bass Inc., Publishers, San Francisco, CA 94104, in association with the ERIC Clearinghouse for Junior Colleges. *New Directions* is numbered sequentially—please order extra copies by sequential number. The volume and issue numbers above are included for the convenience of libraries. Second class postage rates are paid at San Francisco, California, and at additional mailing offices.

The material in this publication was prepared pursuant to a contract with the Office of Educational Research and Improvement, U.S. Department of Education. Contractors undertaking such projects under government sponsorship are encouraged to express freely their judgment in professional and technical matters. Prior to publication, the manuscript was submitted to the Center for the Study of Community Colleges for critical review and determination of professional competence. This publication has met such standards. Points of view or opinions, however, do not necessarily represent the official view or opinions of the Center for the Study of Community Colleges or the Office of Educational Research and Improvement.

Correspondence:
Subscriptions, single-issue orders, change of address notices, undelivered copies, and other correspondence should be sent to Subscriptions, Jossey-Bass Inc., Publishers, 433 California Street, San Francisco, California 94104.

Editorial correspondence should be sent to the Editor-in-Chief, Arthur M. Cohen, at the ERIC Clearinghouse for Junior Colleges, University of California, Los Angeles, California 90024.

Library of Congress Catalog Card Number 85-81881

International Standard Serial Number ISSN 0194-3081

International Standard Book Number ISBN 87589-708-8

Cover art by WILLI BAUM

Manufactured in the United States of America

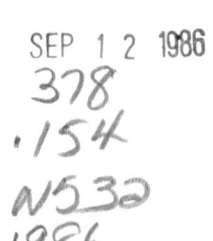

OERI
Office of Educational Research and Improvement
U.S. Department of Education

Ordering Information

The paperback sourcebooks listed below are published quarterly and can be ordered either by subscription or single-copy.

Subscriptions cost $40.00 per year for institutions, agencies, and libraries. Individuals can subscribe at the special rate of $30.00 per year *if payment is by personal check.* (Note that the full rate of $40.00 applies if payment is by institutional check, even if the subscription is designated for an individual.) Standing orders are accepted.

Single copies are available at $9.95 when payment accompanies order, and *all single-copy orders under $25.00 must include payment.* (California, New Jersey, New York, and Washington, D.C., residents please include appropriate sales tax.) For billed orders, cost per copy is $9.95 plus postage and handling. (Prices subject to change without notice.)

Bulk orders (ten or more copies) of any individual sourcebook are available at the following discounted prices: 10-49 copies, $8.95 each; 50-100 copies, $7.96 each; over 100 copies, *inquire.* Sales tax and postage and handling charges apply as for single copy orders.

To ensure correct and prompt delivery, all orders must give either the *name of an individual* or an *official purchase order number.* Please submit your order as follows:

Subscriptions: specify series and year subscription is to begin.
Single Copies: specify sourcebook code (such as, CC1) and first two words of title.

Mail orders for United States and Possessions, Latin America, Canada, Japan, Australia, and New Zealand to:
Jossey-Bass Inc., Publishers
433 California Street
San Francisco, California 94104

Mail orders for all other parts of the world to:
Jossey-Bass Limited
28 Banner Street
London EC1Y 8QE

New Directions for Community Colleges Series
Arthur M. Cohen, *Editor-in-Chief*
Florence B. Brawer, *Associate Editor*

CC1 *Toward a Professional Faculty,* Arthur M. Cohen
CC2 *Meeting the Financial Crisis,* John Lombardi
CC3 *Understanding Diverse Students,* Dorothy M. Knoell
CC4 *Updating Occupational Education,* Norman C. Harris

CC5	*Implementing Innovative Instruction,* Roger H. Garrison
CC6	*Coordinating State Systems,* Edmund J. Gleazer, Jr., Roger Yarrington
CC7	*From Class to Mass Learning,* William M. Birenbaum
CC8	*Humanizing Student Services,* Clyde E. Blocker
CC9	*Using Instructional Technology,* George H. Voegel
CC10	*Reforming College Governance,* Richard C. Richardson, Jr.
CC11	*Adjusting to Collective Bargaining,* Richard J. Ernst
CC12	*Merging the Humanities,* Leslie Koltai
CC13	*Changing Managerial Perspectives,* Barry Heermann
CC14	*Reaching Out Through Community Service,* Hope M. Holcomb
CC15	*Enhancing Trustee Effectiveness,* Victoria Dziuba, William Meardy
CC16	*Easing the Transition from Schooling to Work,* Harry F. Silberman, Mark B. Ginsburg
CC17	*Changing Instructional Strategies,* James O. Hammons
CC18	*Assessing Student Academic and Social Progress,* Leonard L. Baird
CC19	*Developing Staff Potential,* Terry O'Banion
CC20	*Improving Relations with the Public,* Louis W. Bender, Benjamin R. Wygal
CC21	*Implementing Community-Based Education,* Ervin L. Harlacher, James F. Gollattscheck
CC22	*Coping with Reduced Resources,* Richard L. Alfred
CC23	*Balancing State and Local Control,* Searle F. Charles
CC24	*Responding to New Missions,* Myron A. Marty
CC25	*Shaping the Curriculum,* Arthur M. Cohen
CC26	*Advancing International Education,* Maxwell C. King, Robert L. Breuder
CC27	*Serving New Populations,* Patricia Ann Walsh
CC28	*Managing in a New Era,* Robert E. Lahti
CC29	*Serving Lifelong Learners,* Barry Heermann, Cheryl Coppeck Enders, Elizabeth Wine
CC30	*Using Part-Time Faculty Effectively,* Michael H. Parsons
CC31	*Teaching the Sciences,* Florence B. Brawer
CC32	*Questioning the Community College Role,* George B. Vaughan
CC33	*Occupational Education Today,* Kathleen F. Arns
CC34	*Women in Community Colleges,* Judith S. Eaton
CC35	*Improving Decision Making,* Mantha Mehallis
CC36	*Marketing the Program,* William A. Keim, Marybelle C. Keim
CC37	*Organization Development: Change Strategies,* James Hammons
CC38	*Institutional Impacts on Campus, Community, and Business Constituencies,* Richard L. Alfred
CC39	*Improving Articulation and Transfer Relationships,* Frederick C. Kintzer
CC40	*General Education in Two-Year Colleges,* B. Lamar Johnson
CC41	*Evaluating Faculty and Staff,* Al Smith
CC42	*Advancing the Liberal Arts,* Stanley F. Turesky
CC43	*Counseling: A Crucial Function for the 1980s,* Alice S. Thurston, William A. Robbins
CC44	*Strategic Management in the Community College,* Gunder A. Myran
CC45	*Designing Programs for Community Groups,* S. V. Martorana, William E. Piland
CC46	*Emerging Roles for Community College Leaders,* Richard L. Alfred, Paul A. Elsner, R. Jan LeCroy, Nancy Armes
CC47	*Microcomputer Applications in Administration and Instruction,* Donald A. Dellow, Lawrence H. Poole

CC48 *Customized Job Training for Business and Industry,* Robert J. Kopecek, Robert G. Clarke
CC49 *Ensuring Effective Governance,* William L. Deegan, James F. Gollattscheck
CC50 *Strengthening Financial Management,* Dale F. Campbell
CC51 *Active Trusteeship for a Changing Era,* Gary Frank Petty
CC52 *Maintaining Institutional Integrity,* Donald E. Puyear, George B. Vaughan
CC53 *Controversies and Decision Making in Difficult Economic Times,* Billie Wright Dziech

Contents

Editor's Notes 1
L. Steven Zwerling

Chapter 1. From Mass to Class in Higher Education 3
William M. Birenbaum

Can the democratic ideals of America and the spectrum of talents required to sustain the economy be realized at the same time? Can the community college's traditional open door be transformed into a grand doorway through which the disenfranchished can achieve the American dream?

Chapter 2. Community Colleges and Social Stratification 13
in the 1980s
Jerome Karabel

Some individuals who would otherwise have been excluded from higher education have used the community college for upward mobility. Yet the overall impact of the community college has been to accentuate rather than to reduce prevailing patterns of social and class inequality.

Chapter 3. The Devaluation of Transfer: Current Explanations 31
and Possible Causes
Alison Bernstein

Fewer students are transferring to senior colleges, but explanations do not adequately describe this phenomenon. To say that students are less interested misses the point. One must look, therefore, at the institutional impediments to transfer.

Chapter 4. Vocational Education: More False Promises 41
Fred L. Pincus

Even though community colleges are now predominantly vocational-training institutions, vocational programs are more likely to benefit local business interests than the students who participate.

Chapter 5. Lifelong Learning: A New Form of Tracking 53
L. Steven Zwerling

Although community and continuing education currently contribute to social and economic inequality, new approaches can yield more democratic results.

Chapter 6. Minority Students and the Community College 61
Reginald Wilson
Enrollments have declined, failure rates have increased, and federal support has waned. Community colleges, as the access point to higher education for most minority students, have not responded successfully; but they, too, must be understood in the wider context of pervasive societal limitations on upward mobility.

Chapter 7. A Place for Women? 71
Marilyn Gittell
Although women are 60 percent of community college enrollments, there have been few studies of their experiences at two-year colleges. There is evidence to suggest, however, that curricular stereotyping—especially in vocational programs—is a disadvantage to women.

Chapter 8. Independent Students at Two-Year Institutions and the Future of Financial Aid 81
W. Lee Hansen, Jacob O. Stampen
Little is known about how financial aid is distributed among different categories of students. The apparent shift of funds to older, independent students potentially places needier, traditional-age students at comparative risk.

Chapter 9. Strangers to Our Shores 91
Howard B. London
Community colleges play diverse and sometimes contradictory roles for different groups of students. Some students participate in an academic culture of mores that works against academic achievement; others, mostly older students, are quite enthusiastic about the possibilities for upward mobility and broadening their horizons.

Chapter 10. Sources and Information: The Social Role of the Community College 101
Jim Palmer
This chapter draws from the ERIC (Educational Resources Information Center) data base to provide further sources of information on the social role of the community college.

Index 115

Editor's Notes

From the mid-1960s through the mid-1970s there was a lively debate among proponents of the community college movement, as it existed, and a smaller group of critics who challenged many of its fundamental assumptions. To be sure, the proponents found things to criticize, and the "revisionists" responded positively to the democratic possibilities of the system.

During the past decade, however, the critics have been rather silent, while the better-established figures in the field have continued to speak out and to take on the revisionists. Have the critics become quiet as the result of the effectiveness of the counterattack? Is it because they recognize that significant changes have occurred within two-year colleges, so that their critique is no longer valid?

This volume revisits some major critics. Their contributions reveal that their perspectives, while altered, have not undergone radical transformation. They still see the two-year college playing too regressive a role in society, in spite of the continuing democratic rhetoric. In fact, poor people, minorities, and lifelong learners are possibly less well served now than they were a generation ago.

It would appear that many state legislatures have adopted the revisionists' perspective—not because they agree with the underlying analyses, but because they are more and more responsible for paying the bills. As the source of funds has moved from the local community to the state capital, the community college critics' questions of a decade ago are raised: Why are so few students transferring? Are the vaunted vocational programs actually preparing students for jobs? Why are minorities underrepresented? Do you really expect us to spend taxpayers' money for classes in belly dancing?

Ready answers are not always at hand, but, as this volume should indicate, the critics recognize programs that work and believe that community colleges may yet become more effective in helping their students achieve their diverse goals.

This sourcebook is in effect made up of three sections. The first, with chapters by Birenbaum and Karabel, sets the context: the aspirations of American democracy, the various roles of higher education, and the current world of the community college. The second section takes a critical look at each of the traditional functions of the comprehensive two-year college: the collegiate (Bernstein), career (Pincus), and community (Zwerling).

The third section examines the effects of the community college on major student constituencies: minorities (Wilson) and women (Gittell).

This section also explores the effects of financial aid practices (Hansen and Stampen) and the culture of the two-year college (London). The concluding chapter provides sources and information from the ERIC (Educational Resources Information Center) data base (Palmer).

Taken together, these ten chapters update the rich debates that enlivened an earlier era. The critics, it is satisfying to note, remain as lively as the institutions upon which they cast a cold eye. It should be clear also that their criticism does not negate their optimism and their belief in human and institutional possibilities.

L. Steven Zwerling
Editor

L. Steven Zwerling is associate dean of New York University's School of Continuing Education and author of Second Best: The Crisis of the Community College.

Educational institutions whose standards and practices encourage the segregation of people and ideas are unfit to pursue excellence in an open-admissions society.

From Mass to Class in Higher Education

William M. Birenbaum

The Retreat to Excellence

"Two forces shape the mood of our people far more than others now: first, a high technology dominates the economy and generates far-reaching cultural change; and second, the current problems of race and poverty reinvigorate the traditional egalitarian thrust in American society and lay the foundation for many of the most explosive political issues" (Birenbaum, 1973). Today, thirteen years after I formulated these thoughts, these two powerful lines of economic and political development have reached a critical new intersection in American life.

Can the democratic ideals of an open-admissions America and the spectrum of talents required to sustain the nation's rapidly changing economy both be delivered fully at the same time? An all-American answer to this question would naturally be in the affirmative. We have a historic commitment to an equal opportunity for participation by all of our people in the nation's political and economic institutions. In a heterogeneous and pluralistic society, we claim that the release of each person's talents guarantees the creativity and inventiveness underpinning our economic success. We also believe that ever-rising levels of productivity are essential to keeping the doors of opportunity open to all our people. Thus, theoretically, the politics of the democratic ethic and the dynamics of an economy increasingly shaped by science and technology are mutually supportive and should inevitably result in the freest and richest nation yet to exist on the planet.

There is ample evidence, however, that this answer does not quite accurately portray the all-American reality. We confront a demography projecting acute shortages in various skilled manpower categories throughout the balance of this century. We also face the prospect of a growing base of unemployable people distinguished by race, age, and sex. For the first time in our history, Americans over sixty-five outnumber the teenagers. The number of high school graduates will decline by about 20 percent during the next decade. A shrinking pool of eighteen-year-olds will intensify the competition for talent among the private sector, academe, and the military.

At the same time, the nation is absorbing one of the greatest waves of immigration in its history, mostly from Latin America, the Caribbean, and Southeast Asia. Minority groups are the youngest and most rapidly growing element in our population. Today, the average age of blacks in the United States is twenty-five, and of Hispanics, twenty-two, compared with thirty-one among whites. Minorities will comprise more than a third of the census in the year 2000 and in some states, like California, will account for the majority. They and women are becoming the major pool of new talent available at the entry level of the workforce. But today, 13 percent of the white, 43 percent of the black, and more than 50 percent of the Hispanic seventeen-year-olds are functionally illiterate; 13 percent of the nation's high school students are functionally illiterate, as are 60 percent of those who drop out. Our country itself has dropped to forty-ninth among the members of the United Nations in the percent of its citizens who are literate. Chronic unemployment is inevitable under these circumstances and a national tragedy in the light of who is unemployed.

But more than these dreadful data has inspired the recent cascade of critical reports calling for the reform of the nation's educational institutions. The quality of the teaching force, of academic management systems, and of graduate, professional, and undergraduate liberal education all have been challenged, a circumstance extending the critique into academic sectors serving broad middle-class constituencies and the privileged.

It should be no surprise, therefore, to find nonacademic leaders from the professions, commerce and industry, and public life in the forefront of the call for change. Nor is it surprising that the educational establishment is the prime target. Those responsible for economic and public life have a very practical and often self-serving interest in the productivity of the educational institutions. Historically, the educational institutions have played the central role in harmonizing our democratic aspirations with the nation's talent requirements for economic growth. Indeed, the greatest American educational innovations have resulted from this effort.

From Thomas Jefferson's design for the University of Virginia to Lyndon Johnson's proposals written into the Higher Education Act of 1968, these two themes have intertwined. A political theme championed opening admissions to new classes. An economic theme added greater distributive justice to the traditional purposes of formal education. These themes were at the heart of Horace Mann's advocacy of universal public education. They were the essence of the Morrill Act creating the land-grant universities. They inspired the growth of today's community colleges, the adoption of the G.I. Bill after World War II, and the multibillion dollar financial aid programs after 1968.

As I write these words in the spring of 1986, the Dow Jones averages have soared to unprecedented heights, but at least fifteen million Americans remain virtually bypassed after more than forty months of sustained economic strength. These include those unqualified and unable to find jobs; middle-aged workers displaced by the changing job market; high school dropouts, especially young blacks; and many female heads of households. Minority group enrollments and employment in higher education are in decline and disproportionately congeal in the two-year colleges. Urban-suburban lower schools, notwithstanding the legal prohibitions against segregation, are becoming more segregated as a consequence of economic and social realities. The cost of higher education continues to rise at two or three times the rate of inflation, while financial aid appropriations face further sharp cutbacks.

In this climate, an educational reform movement guided by such slogans as "back to the basics" and "raise the standards" may be misunderstood by and damaging to the very people it means to enlist and serve. The importance of mastering the basics, measuring progress according to some standards, and striving for excellence is not at issue. The question is whether these worthy objectives may practically be achieved by going back—back to pitting the value of acquiring knowledge against the value of using it competently; back to the strained and unnatural relationships academe has encouraged between lower and higher education, liberal-general and career-professional education, and formal and experiential education.

The danger is that the slogans popularized by this reform movement may serve only to encourage a retreat to educational premises, methods, and structures that predate the contemporary American situation and are unequal to the political, economic, and cultural challenges this nation faces. This movement could become the first in our educational history to close admissions and widen the growing opportunity gap between the haves and the have-nots in our economy. This would amount to an academic retreat from the reality of how American is becoming—a further distancing of the internal politics and economy of a reactionary academe from the external dynamics of the revolutionary society to which it is reacting.

The Defense of Reaction

Many in higher education deplore the main themes emerging in American life. These themes threaten the validity of the traditional answers they have given both to their professional and political questions. However, technology, urbanization, pluralism, and rapid rates of unpredictable change are not going to go away. The popularization of culture and an extraordinary capacity to know far more than we may ever understand are here to stay.

Information has become a commodity essential to doing almost everything. The manipulation, interpretation, and communication of what is known have become the dominant techniques of politics as well as of economy. This development profoundly changes the context for organized formal education. The colleges and universities are now but one sector in the forefront of the discovery and communication of knowledge. Corporations in the private sector have become formidable competitors in the provision of postsecondary training and education. Nearly $60 billion is spent annually now to support these corporate programs. The corporate programs rely on the new technologies for instructional purposes more extensively than the traditional institutions do and are often more cost-effective and innovative. They range from accredited Ph.D. programs to on-the-job training. Many have a growing appeal to a general constituency beyond corporate employees and represent a vigorous new profit center in the private sector.

It is quixotic, at the very least, for the academic institutions not to recognize that they too are in the learning business. This business involves competition and profit and creates among its clients expectations of success, but such recognition compels a reconsideration of production and marketing techniques intricately interwoven with the self-esteem and pretensions of the colleges and universities. Until lately, they officially have not been especially interested in profit or been challenged seriously about how their own success is to be measured.

The demographics of diversity are a hallmark of how America is becoming. For practical economic and ideological reasons, educational programs in the United States must embrace the heterogeneity of the populations they aim to serve. In this respect, the United States is not Japan, the Federal Republic of Germany, or even the Soviet Union. Educational reform is now a major issue in Japan, Germany, and the Soviet Union and in many other nations. All are unsettled by the tensions between providing education for productive work, in economies increasingly driven by information technologies, and the provision of cultural education, the transmission of a civilization's legacies, a nation's integrity, a culture's excellence. In Japan and Germany and even in the Soviet Union, educators may still assume a framework of commonly shared cultural values and/or a common language and/or a common ideological code as they pursue their dual missions. The designs of liberal, graduate, and professional schools in the United States have long assumed the homogeneity of the populations they serve. This assumption has guided admissions policies that equip the more selective schools to announce proudly that they reject many more than they accept, but this assumption is seriously challenged by what we have become and are becoming. This is a challenge both to the methods and to the content of liberal and career-professional education—what each is about, how each is done, where, and when.

Mobility (not always upward) and change (not always for the better, and usually unpredictable) are implicit in the American situation. People change their jobs and careers, residences, friends, and life-styles with increasing frequency. These changes generate new motivations for learning, multiply the occasions for further education throughout life, and substantially alter the conditions for formal education.

Consider the profile of the twelve million people currently enrolled in the nation's colleges and universities. Two-thirds are commuters, and 50 percent of all the undergraduates are enrolled in the community colleges, which become, therefore, a major if not the only source for whatever "liberal" education these undergraduates receive. Of all of the students, and those who teach them, 40 percent are part-timers. Within five years, at least half of all the students in higher education will be over twenty-five, and more than a fifth will be over thirty-five. Only half who now enroll ever achieve the baccalaureate, and more than half who earn the degree take more than four years to do so. Half attend more than one college in the process of obtaining the degree. Among the secondary school graduates who go on to college, one out of three delays entry by at least one year after high school. Transfers account for more than 40 percent of the enrollments in most undergraduate colleges. The majority of the twelve million are enrolled in large, urban-based institutions. Nearly 80 percent now attend public colleges and universities. In some regions of the country, the number of four-year college graduates who subsequently enroll in two-year colleges for additional credentials exceeds the number of two-year college graduates transferring into the four-year system.

This is not the profile for which the colleges and universities have traditionally designed their curricula, organized their calendars, or planned their campus communities. They have assumed the full-time commitment of their students and employees over a number of years in a rather more than less sequestered "residential" campus "community." Most of the private liberal arts colleges, established during the last century, are isolated geographically from urban population and cultural centers. Curricula have distinguished sharply between "liberal" or cultural education and preparation for careers or professions. The programs generally assume that these are two separate streams, each potentially contaminating the other, and thus best staged sequentially rather than simultaneously. The programs usually assume, whatever the life circumstances of the students, that the undergraduate years are the prime time for the transmission of culture. Finally, while lip service is paid to diversity, admissions and performance standards, curricula, and the organization of campus environments assume the homogeneity of the people involved. Of course, the homogeneity central to these assumptions projects particular class values.

There is a huge gap between these assumptions and the reality of academe's markets in the United States, the expectations of its clienteles, and their behavior in relation to the educational institutions. This gap expresses academe's attitudinal resistance to what is happening in the society it is supposed to serve. More and more people are improvising accommodations of their practical educational needs in this culture as it is becoming. The information-electronic economy readily implements their improvisations, many of which are outside the traditional academic sector. Within academe, the adult, continuing, and special-education programs that try to capitalize on this reality are often organized and administered beyond the mainstream, as second-rate enterprises.

The Liberal Arts: Work Befitting a Free Person

The main themes in American life reflect substantial changes in the responsibilities of citizenship, the attitudes of people toward self-fulfillment, and the terms for successful participation in the economy. The terms and conditions for employment powerfully illustrate these changes.

Less than a third of the American workforce is now employed in the traditional categories of industrial production—agriculture and manufacturing. Automation—the use of robots and computers—and the continued attraction of cheap labor abroad will further reduce the number of these jobs. More than two-thirds of the jobs are now in the service sector, and it is mainly there that the new jobs will appear.

The U.S. Bureau of Labor Statistics estimates that virtually all the jobs to be done in the 1990s will require some training or education beyond the secondary level. The majority of these jobs do not and will not require mastery of the sophisticated levels of the new technologies, but most will require people to work with and serve each other directly.

The new technologies encourage both decentralization of decision making and greater worker participation in the process. The morale of the workers is a decisive factor in the delivery of the human services. These jobs place a premium on interpersonal and organizational talents. These talents require educated capacities not only to communicate but also to exercise judgment.

The mastery of language, numbers, and the use of electronic systems is essential in modern communications, but something more than these "basic skills" is basic. Judgment is exercised not only in terms of the immediate task to be done but also in the context of human experience and intellect, guided by an understanding of the history and social environment of a culture. Access to enriched life experience and cultural education are crucial to the exercise of civilized judgment.

The new technologies change the landscape for doing business and for working. For example, in a crucial part of the economy they internationalize decisions concerning the use of land and access to labor—where to locate, how to mobilize capital, and how to organize and manage. All of this changes the educational agenda of those who work and lead—what they need to know in order to decide and function. Never before has doing business been so enmeshed in public policy processes and in the negotiation of diverse and conflicting cultural values. The responsibilities and accountability of the decision makers are changed. These changes bear directly on the attitudes of those affected by the decisions.

The modern workplace is a major arena in which people exercise judgment and communicate not only about the job itself but also about the political and cultural relationships that naturally engulf the job. It is a premiere stage, on which the officially stated benefits of a liberal education and the practical and often specialized capacities to do a job combine in a dramatic performance, and this performance is almost always staged before very critical audiences.

A high school diploma is the sine qua non for limited employability and access to the American stage. Even the liberal arts degree alone leaves large numbers who achieve it either unemployable or unable to apply productively the methodologies for thinking and the formal knowledge acquired. Many programs, narrowly designed to convey skills relevant to a specialized job or career, circumscribe students' ability to progress in this changing economy. Worse, too often they warp students' effective participation in the politics and culture of the workplace and the larger society. Too many graduate and professional programs encourage a disconnection between learning something special and contending with the value-laden issues that invariably attend applying practically what is specially known.

Under these circumstances, each part of the overall system is tempted to point an accusatory finger at the others: The lower schools are failing to equip the students with the basic skills; the community college programs are dead-ended; the senior colleges seem determined to isolate themselves further from the impact of the main events in American life; the graduate and professional schools, serving only those who have survived the prior levels of the system and thus seem destined to manage the main events, have simply sold out to the status quo. Finally, in a rare show of unity, everyone argues that the system at all levels is victimized by the larger societal and cultural forces beyond its control: the breakdown of family life, drugs, racism, crime, and so on.

The liberal arts consist of three components: work, freedom, and personality. The concept of work befitting a free person uniquely encompasses economy, polity, and culture. These are the indispensable ingredients for the education of all Americans, however the various stages of that education may be designated, staged over time and in space, or rationalized in terms of particular institutional jurisdictions and missions.

Nevertheless, in defiance of the nation's ideological commitment to an open-admissions society, and in reaction to external pressures that disturb academe's professional habits and attitudes, higher education has organized to stress the separateness of these three components. This policy magnifies jurisdictional and territorial problems in the organization of education. It subverts the ability of the institutions to practice what they preach about the basics, standards, and excellence.

As the main themes in American life unfold, the nation's colleges and universities are in the middle of their own late-twentieth-century metamorphosis. Three powerful and irreversible forces motivate their transformation. The first is the democratic thrust of the American people, inspired by their diversity and unique historical experience. The second is utility—the popular conviction and practical necessity that higher education should contribute toward economic stability in peace and toward security in war. The third is science and technology—their centrality to achieving economic health and to the production and communication of knowledge.

The combination of these forces sets the stage for the reformation of education, for life and for making a living, and for the reconciliation of economy, polity, and culture in the educational opportunities provided for a diverse American population.

Filters

The role the community colleges play on this stage reflects the ambiguity of how they were originally cast. They arose out of two very different lines of thought. One held that the first two years of the undergraduate college were essentially comparable to the last two years of secondary education in the European systems. Since they were seen as extensions of the secondary schools, some welcomed the two-year colleges as devices to keep the university itself pure, within the terms of elitist European traditions. The second line of thought saw the two-year colleges as grand doorways through which Everyman would pass en route to his own realization of the American dream. These were to be the people's colleges, to serve the communities where the people lived, to emphasize teaching, and to provide educational opportunity for large numbers of Americans denied direct entry into the traditional colleges and universities.

Elements of both these positions are present in what the community colleges have become. For millions of students, they are indeed a doorway, but they also serve as filters for the senior system. To keep their doors open—to remain respectable filters—they are pressured to honor the curricular values and styles of those very colleges that originally rejected many of the students whom they admit. Praised for their openness, they are criticized for creating the consequences of being open. The senior colleges, eager to embrace the cream of the two-year college crop, count on them to be effective filters, but at some point filters close the doors of opportunity for those who are filtered.

This ambiguity complicates and usually frustrates any serious negotiation between the community colleges and the senior colleges, just as it subverts treaty making between the lower and higher, undergraduate and graduate, and academic and nonacademic sectors of education. It also underscores that academic tendency in the pursuit of excellence—to dwell excessively on the destination, at the expense of the trip. Once an institution at any level in the system becomes obsessed by the defense of its own goals, standards, and programs, it readily retreats from the fundamental and substantial problems that transcend its goals, programs, and standards.

The academy, reacting to current pressures to change, concentrates on the affirmation of traditional goals and a more rigorous application of "standards" to buttress programmatic destinations in which its self-interests are already deeply vested. In a very real sense, higher education is just hanging in. It measures the quality of its leaders by their capacity to manage survival.

We are in a climate of reform distressingly unmarked by passionate storms. Quite the opposite: In an oppressive and ominous calm, we are organizing to march forward to the good old days, a long march of retreat from the pursuit of our ideals.

In the pursuit of excellence, the destination is less a glistening city, beckoning on the shores of some distant graduation day, than a misty mirage, an ever-changing and mysterious possibility luring us on. This is a trip across largely uncharted waters. Never before have the inventions of science and technology washed so extensively over virtually all the subject matter of education—the generation of knowledge, its storage and recall, the transmission of information, the methods for learning. Never before have such inventions framed such difficult and far-reaching political issues, philosophical choices, and economic dilemmas and opportunities. Never before have their operations permeated and changed culture so deeply.

Pervasive new relationships between technology and science and between science and the humanities argue powerfully for a fundamental redefinition of liberal education, of its content as well as its methods. The economic implications of these new relationships focus on the processes, the terms, and the conditions for productive work. Thus, the redefinition of liberal education must penetrate the barriers that have grown to separate it from education for productive work.

The colleges and universities stand astride this critical new intersection that the main lines of economic and political development have reached in American life. At this dangerous but fascinating juncture, at least one thing is clear: Educational institutions whose standards and practices encourage the segregation of people and ideas are unfit to pursue excellence in an open-admissions society.

Reference

Birenbaum, W. M. "From Class to Mass in Higher Education." In W. M. Birenbaum (Ed.), *From Class to Mass Learning.* New Directions for Community Colleges, no. 7. San Francisco: Jossey-Bass, 1974.

William M. Birenbaum served as the president of the Staten Island Community College from 1968 to 1976 and of Antioch University from 1976 to 1985. Currently he is the president of Corporate/Education Strategies, a consulting firm in New York City.

Developments in American community colleges since 1972 combine to demonstrate that these institutions must renew their commitment to the community college's historic link with four-year colleges.

Community Colleges and Social Stratification in the 1980s

Jerome Karabel

In 1971, amidst the political and social upheavals then shaking American higher education, I began research on the relationship of the rapidly expanding community college to larger patterns of social inequality. Then, as now, I was not alone in my effort to understand the role of the educational system as a source of both stability and change; indeed, Bowles and Gintis had already begun to publish some of the critical empirical and theoretical inquiries that would culminate in the appearance of *Schooling in Capitalist America* (1976) and Collins (1971) published a seminal article that foreshadowed many of the themes that he would develop in *The Credential Society* (1979). Given its extraordinary rate of growth and its obvious relevance to the process of stratification, the community college has received surprisingly little attention from social scientists; indeed, in the decade after Burton Clark's classic *The Open-Door College* appeared in 1960, not a single major work by a social scientist was published that focused exclusively on the community college. The work that did appear was primarily, although not exclusively, by people who were in one way or another associated with the community college. While, at its best, such work was extremely illuminating, much of it suffered from a lack of detachment. It was not until the early and middle 1970s, in a changed political climate, that a group of university-based individuals whom Oromaner (1983) has called "outsiders" began to publish a series of critical works on the community college. As Oromaner has pointed out, neither "insiders" nor "outsiders" are immune to the characteristic biases and distortions associated with their positions in the social structure.

My own interest in the community college was based on my belief that it constituted an important, albeit somewhat neglected, segment of the educational system—one that embodied, I suspected, many of the contradictions of the characteristically American search for social salvation through education. Influenced by the wave of "revisionist" scholarship that was beginning to overturn established interpretations of the history and character of American schooling, yet at the same time personally committed to reform as a means of realizing the democratic potential of educational expansion, I set out to examine systematically the institution that was becoming the principle point of entry into higher education for previously excluded working-class and minority youths: the community college. The results of my investigation were published in an article titled "Community Colleges and Social Stratification" (Karabel, 1972).

The thesis of this article was that "the community college, generally viewed as the leading edge of an open and egalitarian system of higher education, is in reality a prime contemporary expression of the dual historical patterns of class-based tracking and educational inflation." Moreover, I suggested, tracking takes place within the community college in the form of vocational education. Because of its place in a larger system of educational and social stratification, the two-year college was a site of "submerged class conflict" (Karabel, 1972, p. 526). Far from increasing the rate of social mobility or the level of economic equality, the expansion of the community college, I argued, contributed to the reproduction of existing patterns of social and economic inequality (see also Karabel, 1974).

This thesis was a controversial one, and—along with the arguments of other critics of community colleges, such as Pincus (1974, 1980), Zwerling (1976), and London (1978)—it has been subjected to serious and sustained criticism. The aforementioned scholars by no means exhaust the list of critics of community colleges. A more comprehensive list would include Wilms (1974), Astin (1982, 1984), Grubb (1984), and Dougherty (1986a, 1986b). While these individuals by no means agree on every particular, they share a common skepticism about the community college's claims to have democratized higher education and substantially expanded opportunities for upward mobility for subordinate classes and racial minorities. Among the major responses to the claims of the critics are those of Clark (1980), Riesman (1980), and Cohen and Brawer (1982).

In the limited space available here, I wish to concentrate less on responding to those with opposing views that on reporting some of the key findings of research on community colleges since 1972 and discussing some of the major changes that have taken place in these institutions in recent years. (The major community college development in recent years—the growing prominence of vocational programs—is treated in depth in a book manuscript, tentatively titled *The Transformation of the Community College,* and currently being prepared by Brint and Karabel for Oxford University Press. While this issue will be touched on very briefly in the pages that follow, readers interested in the causes of growing vocationalism may wish to consult our forthcoming volume.) I will conclude with an examination of some of the outstanding issues that researchers need to address, and a few brief reflections on current dilemmas facing the community college.

Key Findings from Recent Research

In making the case that community colleges, rather than improving the mobility prospects of members of subordinate groups, had instead had the overall effect of reproducing existing class and racial differences, I drew on empirical evidence about the social composition of community colleges, the effects of these institutions on persistence in higher education, and the impact of attendance at a two-year college on subsequent position in the labor market. The underlying logic of the argument consisted of three distinct but related propositions: that community colleges constituted the bottom track of higher education's class-based system of interinstitutional stratification; that attending a community college had the independent effect of reducing the probability that a given individual would obtain a bachelor's degree; and that among otherwise similar individuals (in terms of social background and academic ability), the impact of attending a two-year college, as opposed to a four-year college, on later income and occupational status was negative.

If all three of these propositions were true, then the growth of open-access community colleges, I argued, had the paradoxical effect of accentuating existing class differences, for the very institutions that were enrolling a disproportionately high number of working-class and minority students had the most negative effects of all types of colleges and universities on the educational and occupational life chances of those individuals who passed through them. The argument was not that the community college failed to serve as a ladder of upward mobility for some individuals, but rather than in the aggregate its expansion had the effect of reproducing existing class differences.

Community colleges have, of course, made college attendance possible for some individuals who would otherwise never have enrolled in higher education. But Tinto (1975), in an important article on the distributive effects of public two-year college availability, finds that the presence of a community college may do less to increase rates of college attendance than to alter the type of college attended. The availability of a community college, Tinto argues, leads lower- and middle-status persons to substitute attendance at a two-year institution for attendance at a four-year institution. To the extent that this substitution effect diverts individuals from nonprivileged backgrounds away from four-year institutions, the expansion of community colleges may paradoxically lead to an increase in inequality of educational opportunity, for, as we shall see, attendance at a two- rather than a four-year institution has a negative independent effect on the likelihood of completing a bachelor's degree.

My concern in 1972 was to explain how "educational inflation" permitted the system of higher education to expand without narrowing relative differences between groups or changing the underlying structure of opportunity. Within this framework, it was expected that some individuals would use the two-year college as a launching pad for upward mobility; indeed, such cases were seen as tending to legitimate prevailing patterns of educational and social selection. In another context, the French sociologist Bourdieu (1977, p. 487), a leading proponent of "reproduction" theory, has made the same point with characteristic elegance: "the controlled mobility of a limited category of individuals . . . is not incompatible with the permanence of structure, and . . . is even capable of contributing to social stability in the only way conceivable in societies based upon democratic ideals."

The first proposition—that community colleges constitute the bottom track of the system of higher education's structure of interinstitutional stratification—has now been replicated so many times that it is no longer controversial. Whether one is referring to parental income, occupational status, or educational attainment, nineteen consecutive surveys of college freshmen by the American Council of Education (in recent years, in cooperation with the Higher Education Research Institute of UCLA) have confirmed that the social composition of the two-year colleges is lower than that of four-year colleges, which in turn rank below universities. In 1984, for example, the proportion of students from families with incomes less than $25,000 at two-year colleges, four-year colleges, and universities was 48.3 percent, 39.9 percent, and 28.7 percent, respectively. Similarly, the proportion of students whose mothers had never attended college was 69.4 percent, 56.2 percent, and 44.7 percent (Astin and others, 1984, p. 51). Findings from national longitudinal studies of the high school classes of 1972 and 1980 conducted by the National Center for Educational Statistics (NCES) point in similar directions (NCES, 1985, p. 224).

The second proposition—that (controlling for individual differences) attending a community college had a negative effect on a student's likelihood of obtaining a bachelor's degree—was controversial when it was first put forward and remains so today; yet those studies that have addressed the issue in the intervening years have consistently supported the original generalization that otherwise similar students (in terms of educational aspirations, social background, academic ability, and other relevant individual characteristics) are more likely to complete the B.A. if they initially enroll in four-year institutions. The accumulation of data on this point constitutes one of the most impressive advances in research on community colleges in recent years. Indeed, sophisticated follow-up studies of large cohorts of entering college students suggest that the question now is not whether attending a community college has a negative impact on persistence in higher education but rather how large is this effect (Alba and Lavin, 1981; Anderson, 1981; Astin, 1982; and Velez, 1985)? (For an illuminating, albeit tentative, discussion of some of the possible reasons why community colleges have negative effects on persistence in higher education, see Dougherty, 1986.)

These differences between two- and four-year college students in likelihood of acquiring a bachelor's degree are therefore not simply artifacts of the undeniably real differences in academic ability, level of educational ambition, and socioeconomic background; even controlling for such factors, sizable negative effects persist. Thus, it is worth reiterating that "tracking in higher education leads to disproportionately high attendance of low-status students at community colleges, which in turn, decreases the likelihood they will stay in school" (Karabel, 1972, p. 536). From the perspective of equality of opportunity, the implications of this pattern of overrepresentation—one in which individuals from working-class and minority backgrounds tend to be concentrated in the very institutions that offer them the least chance of obtaining a bachelor's degree—are sobering. The importance of college completion for nonwhites is highlighted by a finding from the works of Jencks and others (1979): The relative advantage in occupational status of whites over nonwhites is lowest among college graduates; "college graduation is more valuable to nonwhites than whites" (p. 174).

The final proposition—that the independent effects of attending a two-year college versus a four-year college on income and occupational status are negative—was the least well documented of the three. While there was some evidence available in 1972 that college prestige was associated with adult socioeconomic status, no direct evidence was available on the labor market effects of community college attendance. In the years since, however, two noteworthy longitudinal studies have been conducted on this very question. Monk-Turner (1983) found that ten years after high school graduation, four-year college entrants held jobs of higher status, even when controls were introduced for differences in socioeconomic background, measured mental ability, and other variables. Interestingly, this "occupational penalty" associated with attendance at a two-year college was not just a consequence of the negative impact of community colleges or educational attainment but held even among individuals with the same number of years of education. Breneman and Nelson (1981), in a study that must be interpreted somewhat more cautiously than Monk-Turner's because it focuses on individuals just four years out of high school, found that attending a community college had a negative effect on the occupational status of young men and no significant effect on wages. "Because occupational status is generally found to be highly correlated with adult earnings," they conclude, "this positive effect of attending a university (or negative effect of community college attendance) bodes ill for future earnings for those who choose a community college instead of a university right after high school" (p. 86).

The research that has been conducted since 1972 on community colleges, although stronger on some subjects than on others, has thus generally tended to confirm the "revisionist" perspective. With a far greater body of empirical evidence now available, the fundamental argument may be stated again with even greater confidence: Far from embodying the democratization of higher education and a redistribution of opportunity in the wider society, the expansion of the community college instead heralded the arrival in higher education of a form of class-linked tracking that served to reproduce existing social relations. To be sure, some individuals who would otherwise have been excluded from higher education have used the community college as a platform for upward mobility; this may have been the case, in particular, for many adult women who returned to the educational system via the two-year college. Yet, such cases to the contrary notwithstanding, the overall impact of the community college has been to accentuate rather than reduce prevailing patterns of social and class inequality.

New Developments in the Community College

In 1972, I predicted that if current trends continued, "vocational training may well become more pervasive, and the community college will become even more a terminal rather than a transfer institution" (Karabel, 1972, p. 556). While both these predictions have been borne out by subsequent events, others were not. Extrapolating from then-current events, I predicted, for example, an increasingly rigid tracking system. What happened instead was that the community college vocational track, which historically had been a terminal one, came increasingly to be a supplier of transfers to four-year institutions. This was but one of a number of developments that it was not possible to foresee from the vantage point of the time. In reviewing some of the major developments of the period, let us then examine what has—and has not—happened to the community colleges since 1972.

A force shaping every other development in community colleges in recent years has been their extraordinary rate of growth in enrollment. (Some of the figures used in this chapter occasionally lump together all two-year colleges, both public and private, whereas the term *community college* should refer only to public two-year institutions. Since, however, approximately 95 percent of all two-year college students are at public institutions, occasional reliance on such figures should not greatly affect the results.) Between 1970 and 1982, the number of students enrolled in two-year colleges grew from 2,223,000 to 4,772,000—a rate of increase of 215 percent. During the same period, undergraduate enrollment at four-year institutions increased less than 18 percent, from 5,153,000 to 6,053,000 (calculated from NCES, 1985, p. 98). By 1983, over 43 percent of all undergraduates were enrolled at community colleges; among first-time college freshmen, both full- and part-time, over 53 percent (1,308,268) were enrolled in two-year colleges (calculated from fall 1983 Enrollment in *The Chronicle of Higher Education,* January 23, 1985). (If one is referring to the proportion of full-time college freshmen who have proceeded to college directly out of high school, the proportion of students enrolled in two-year colleges is, of course, somewhat lower. In 1972, the proportion of such students was around 35 percent; by 1980, it had increased slightly to about 37 percent, as calculated from NCES, 1985, p. 224.)

Accompanying this remarkable growth has been a change in the character of the student body at community colleges. In comparison to 1972, students at two-year colleges are somewhat older, lower in measured academic ability, more female, and increasingly part-time (Cohen and Brawer, 1982, pp. 29-65). The proportion who attend the two-year college on a part-time basis has undergone a particularly sharp increase in recent years; between 1972 and 1982, it grew from 51 percent to 63 percent (Cohen, 1984, p. 37).

Two-year colleges play an especially important role in serving as gates of entry into higher education for minorities, particularly blacks, Hispanics, and American Indians (Olivas, 1979; Astin, 1982). Data from 1978 reveal considerable overrepresentation of minorities at two-year as opposed to four-year colleges; while only 33.2 percent of all white students were enrolled at two-year public institutions, the figures for blacks, Hispanics, and American Indians were, respectively, 39.3, 53.3, and 53.0 percent (Astin, 1982, p. 131). Given the concentration of Hispanics in California, Texas, and Florida—all states with large community college systems—the importance of the two-year institution for their educational and career opportunities is manifest. And blacks, although not so overrepresented in community colleges as Hispanics and American Indians, are increasingly concentrated there; between 1976 and 1982, the number of blacks enrolled in two-year colleges increased by 60,200, in comparison to an increase of only 8,300 at four-year institutions (NCES, 1985, p. 106).

In terms of the probability that students of different socioeconomic status will attend two-year colleges directly after high school, little change has occurred in recent years. According to a study comparing the high school classes of 1972 and 1980, the likelihood that a student will enroll in a two-year institution was greatest if he or she were from the middle or upper layers of the stratification system; attending a four-year college is most likely, however, for students from the higher levels of the class structure (see Table 1). Whereas students from all three groups were all more likely to attend four-year rather than two-year institutions, the ratio varied sharply by socioeconomic status; thus, in 1980, students of high socioeconomic status were almost three times as likely to attend four-year rather than two-year colleges, in comparison to a ratio of one in thirteen for students from low socioeconomic backgrounds.

The Rise of Vocational Education and the Decline of Transfer

The most striking development in community colleges in recent years has been the extraordinarily rapid rise in vocational education. I estimated (Karabel, 1972) that no more than one-third of two-year college students were enrolled in vocational programs; by 1975, Grubb and Lazerson (1975) already placed the figure at around 50 percent; and Pincus (this volume), drawing on Grubb (1984), suggests that the proportion of community college students in vocational programs is now more than two-thirds. This transformation from an institution primarily offering college-parallel liberal arts programs to one emphasizing terminal vocational programs—a transformation that occurred in little more than a decade—is the most fundamental change to have occurred in the history of the American community college.

The growth in vocational enrollments at the two-year college occurred, of course, in the context of a declining labor market for gradu-

Table 1. College Participation Rates of High School Graduates Immediately Following Graduation, by Socioeconomic Status, Fall 1972 and Fall 1980

	Percent Participating in Fall 1972			*Percent Participating in Fall 1980*		
	Four-Year Institution	*Two-Year Institution*	*Four-Year/ Two-Year Ratio*	*Four-Year Institution*	*Two-Year Institution*	*Four-Year/ Two-Year Ratio*
Low SES	14	11	1.27	17	15	1.13
Middle SES	25	18	1.39	30	19	1.58
High SES	57	18	3.17	55	19	2.89

Source: NCES, 1985, p. 224.

ates of four-year colleges, especially in the liberal arts (Freeman, 1976; Rumberger, 1981). This decline was in turn associated with the leveling off of the process of "educational inflation"—a development that I did not fully foresee in 1972. The number of bachelor's degrees awarded nationally peaked at 945,776 in 1973-1974, dropping to 919,549 in 1976-1977 and remaining near that level for the remainder of the decade (NCES, 1985, p. 124). (Another indication of the leveling off of "educational inflation" is that a rough estimate of the proportion of eighteen-year-olds who later received bachelor's degrees, based on the number of eighteen-year-olds divided by the number of B.A.s awarded four years later, peaked in 1974 at 25 percent, dropped to 21.6 percent in 1979, and rose only slightly to 22.4 percent in 1982.) In contrast, the associate's degree (A.A.)—the diploma most commonly conferred by the community college—rose from under 300,000 in 1971-1972 to over 400,000 by 1976-1977. Within the category of A.A., the proportion of degrees conferred in occupational programs, as opposed to arts and sciences or general programs, rose from over two in five to more than three in five (see Table 2).

But the rise in vocationalism at the community college cannot be understood solely as a consequence of the declining market position of college graduates and the corresponding rise in the popularity of vocational programs. Well before the labor market downturn that began to manifest itself in the early 1970s, powerful forces both inside and outside the community college were pushing (as I argued in 1972) to expand drastically the role of vocational programs. To be sure, objective changes in the labor market prospects of college graduates were occurring, and these changes played a

Table 2. Associate Degrees Conferred by Institutions of Higher Education by Type of Curriculum, 1970-1971 to 1979-1980

Year	All Curricula	Arts and Sciences or General Programs Number	Percentage of Total	Occupational Programs Number	Percentage of Total
1970-71	252,610	144,883	57.4	107,727	42.6
1971-72	292,119	158,283	54.2	133,836	45.8
1972-73	317,008	161,051	50.8	155,957	49.2
1974-75	360,171	166,567	46.2	193,604	53.8
1975-76	391,454	175,185	44.8	216,269	55.2
1976-77	406,377	171,631	42.2	234,746	57.8
1977-78	412,246	167,036	40.5	245,210	59.5
1978-79	402,702	157,572	39.1	245,130	60.9
1979-80	400,910	154,282	38.5	246,626	61.5

Source: Cohen (1984).

crucial role in stimulating the growth of occupational enrollments in the community college; but vocationalism in the two-year college also grew in response to the efforts of community college administrators who, in pursuing their own organizational interests in carving out a distinct niche and identity for their institutions in the complex and highly competitive ecology of American higher education, pushed hard for vocational programs. The role of the community college in sponsoring vocationalism, not just in response to pressure from powerful external forces but in pursuit of its own organizational interests, was not adequately grasped in Karabel (1972), and this constitutes a serious omission. While my assertion that "there was little popular clamor for community college vocational programs" was correct, as was my argument that various institutional elites favored vocationalism, I somewhat inflated the role of big business in pushing for expanded vocational training (subsequent research has revealed widespread corporate indifference to community colleges through 1970) and neglected the role of the community college in vocationalizing itself. The role of the pursuit of organizational interests as a source of structural change in higher education has received considerable attention in my recent works (Karabel, 1983, 1984). With respect to the history of community colleges and the rise of vocational education within them, the theme of organizational interests is pursued in detail in Brint and Karabel (in preparation).

Studies on what happens in the labor market to students enrolled in community college vocational education, although still fragmentary, are much more available than they were in 1972. The results of these studies, while less than definitive, raise serious questions about whether a purely economic model, based on rational choice, can adequately account for the burgeoning enrollments in occupational programs. Pincus (1980), in a thorough review of studies published in the 1970s, finds that a substantial minority of vocational graduates do not even get jobs in the fields for which they were trained, and that economic returns are generally quite modest. Wilms and Hansell (1982), in a follow-up study of vocational graduates in six occupational programs, also find frequent employment in unrelated areas and weak economic returns; in addition, they find that the programs most successful in placing their graduates tend to be those that place them in low-status jobs. While space limitations do not permit a more thorough review of the evidence, it seems that existing studies do not support the claims of advocates that vocational education is, in general, a pathway to upward mobility and economic security. This is not to suggest that no vocational programs yield, in the aggregate, relatively high returns; community college occupational programs are themselves stratified; and some of them, particularly in the health professions and certain technical areas, seem linked to segments of the labor market with reasonably high levels of pay. For the claim that many vocational programs outrank liberal arts programs both in the quality of students and in economic returns, see Riesman (1980), Templin and Shearon (1980), and Cohen and Brawer (1982).

The rapid increase in vocational enrollments is doubtless associated with the striking decline in the rate of transfer from two-year to four-year colleges that has been observed in recent years (Lombardi, 1979), but the relationship between the two is complex. In contrast to 1972, when vocational programs were almost always terminal programs, vocational curricula now sometimes lead to transfer into four-year institutions. The extent to which such transfers occur is unknown, but in some states they seem to be fairly widespread; according to Lombardi (1979, p. 4), in the late 1970s, 36 percent of the associate's degree transfers to the California State University system had occupationally oriented majors, and in New York State in 1974 the comparable figure was 30 percent. While no study claims that the rate of transfer to four-year institutions is now higher from community college vocational programs that it is from college-parallel liberal arts programs, the proportion of two-year college transfers who have been enrolled in vocational curricula may be considerable. Whatever the precise figures, the very fact that significant numbers of students in occupationally oriented curricula can transfer to four-year institutions an important blurring of the historic boundary between community college vocational and liberal arts tracks.

If nothing precise is known about the proportion of vocational students nationwide who are eligible for transfer to four-year colleges, the same may be said for the rate of transfer itself. (For a useful discussion of the numerous problems involved in counting the number of transfer students, see Cohen, 1979.) Nevertheless, all observers (Lombardi, 1979; Friedlander, 1980; Center for the Study of Community Colleges, 1985; Bernstein, this volume) seem to agree that it has declined substantially during the past fifteen to twenty years. In 1972, basing my estimate on data primarily from the 1960s, I stated that no more than 25 to 35 percent of community college students ever transferred to four-year institutions. Lombardi (1979), in an extensive review of statewide studies from the 1970s, estimated that the nationwide rate of transfer for community college students had dropped under 10 percent.

If national-level data are sparse, evidence on transfer rates in California—the state with by far the largest number of students enrolled in community colleges (enrolling roughly one-fourth of all two-year college students nationwide)—is relatively abundant. Moreover, California's three-tiered system of higher education—with community colleges at the bottom (referred to as CCC), California State University (referred to as CSUC) in the middle, and the University of California (UC) at the top—has, at least since the appearance of the renowned Master Plan for Higher Education of 1960, served as model for other states. For these reasons, data on rates of transfer from California community colleges are of special interest.

The data on California suggest a decline in the rate of transfer in recent years, especially to the top tier. Transfers to the University of California peaked in 1973 at 8,193 but dropped to 5,303 in 1983. During the same years, however, the number of transfers to California State University declined only slightly, from 33,089 to 30,274 (see Table 3). What is striking here, in addition to the overall decline in the number of transfers, is the trend in the distribution of transfers by segment. Thus, whereas in 1973 there were slightly more than four transfers to CSUC for every transfer to UC, the ratio had risen to almost six to one by 1983.

It is worth noting that the percentages in Table 3 exclude part-time community college students; had they been included, the percentages would have been substantially lower. At the same time, however, it should also be observed that a calculation using CCC freshmen, rather than all full-time CCC students, would have yielded higher transfer rates. As Lombardi's (1979) review of the literature makes clear, there is no generally agreed-upon technique for calculating the proportion of community college students who transfer to four-year institutions. Whatever the definition used, however, it is unlikely that the trend in rates of transfer revealed in Table 3 would be substantially different.

In a system such as California's, in which over 40 percent of recent high school graduates become freshmen in community colleges, compared to roughly 9 percent and 6 percent at CSUC and UC, respectively, the issue of who ultimately transfers is a crucial one. While evidence on the class composition of transfers is not easily available, data on the racial composition of transfers have been gathered. The results are consistent with the "revisionist" view of the two-year colleges. Whereas blacks and Chicanos constituted 10.1 and 16.7 percent, respectively, of first-time CCC freshmen under age nineteen in 1981, they comprised only 6.6 and 9.7 percent of the transfers to CSUC, and 4.2 and 8.9 percent of transfers to

Table 3. First-Time, Fall-Enrolled Transfer Students
from California Community Colleges to UC and CSUC,
as a Percentage of Full-Time Community College Students
Two Years Prior

Year	Number to UC	Percent to UC	Number to CSUC	Percent to CSUC
1971–1973	8193	2.7	33,089	11.1
1973–1975	8002	2.6	35,537	11.9
1975–1977	6392	1.6	34,001	9.1
1977–1979	5649	1.8	30,428	9.5
1979–1981	4778	1.7	30,026	10.6
1981–1983	5305	1.7	30,274	9.7

Source: California Postsecondary Education Commission, 1984, p. B-4.

UC, in 1983. At some institutions, the racial discrepancies in rates of transfer reached striking proportions; thus, at Laney College in Oakland, whites constituted only 18.9 percent of freshmen but comprised 38.99 percent of transfers to CSUC and 74.2 percent of transfers to UC (California Postsecondary Education Commission, 1984).

Both the national and the California data indicate, then, that by the early 1980s the community college, as I predicted in 1972, had become increasingly cut off from the mainstream of higher education. Increasingly vocational in orientation, community colleges came to emphasize their college-parallel liberal arts programs less and less. At some community colleges, the flow of transfer students slowed to a trickle, and there was talk in policy-making circles of formally eliminating liberal arts transfer programs at institutions where they were already in serious disarray (see McCartan, 1983). To be sure, some students were transferring to four-year colleges from the newly renovated vocational programs; but for most of the students (many of them minority and working-class) who came to the community college in search of opportunity, higher education's bottom track is even more of a dead end today than it was in 1972.

Concluding Remarks

In reflecting on stability and change in the community college since 1972, I am struck by the complexity, for researchers and policy makers alike, of the issues raised by this institution. Space does not permit a detailed treatment of these issues, but I would like to conclude, first, by attempting to identify some priority areas of research and, second, by briefly addressing what I think is the major dilemma facing community colleges today: the fate of their increasingly precarious academic transfer programs. By grouping research and policy issues together, I do not, however, wish to suggest any direct or simple connection between the two; on the contrary, as my priorities on research will make clear, I believe that the process of research must have autonomy from the immediate needs of policy makers if it is to ask the large questions that, in the long run, will raise the level of debate about important issues.

Toward an Agenda for Research. While much more is known now about community colleges and their effects than was the case in 1972, a number of important issues remain unresolved. Among some of the most crucial are:

1. What are the effects of attending a community college on individual life chances in the labor market, as compared to not attending college at all? While much research (my own included) has tended to compare similar individuals who attended two-year as opposed to four-year colleges, what would a comparison with those who never entered the system of higher education reveal?

2. What are the long-term economic returns to different types of vocational education? The vocational track is an extremely heterogeneous one, training registered nurses as well as cosmetologists. What is vocational education's structure of internal stratification, and what are the effects of various programs?

3. Do community colleges have different effects on different kinds of people? A disaggregated approach would not assume that effects are homogeneous across differences of class, race, gender, and age, but would ask such questions as: Are community colleges more valuable to middle-class women trying to re-enter the labor force than they are to working-class women? Does vocational education yield better returns to mature adults who already have jobs but wish to upgrade them than to young people who hope that vocational training will give them entry to secure, well-paid jobs?

4. What is the current transfer rate from two-year to four-year colleges? Which four-year institutions do two-year college transfers enter? Which students—by class, race, and gender—succeed in transferring?

5. Do different state structures of higher education make a difference in the distribution of opportunity? Do states with large systems of community colleges, such as California, have higher class differentials in rates of college completion than states with small community college systems, such as Indiana? Do states with specialized upper-division institutions, such as Florida, have higher rates of transfer than states that do not?

6. What are the effects of community colleges on educational and occupational aspirations? Does the "cooling out" process succeed in limiting the ambition of those who do not succeed in transferring to four-year colleges? To what extent do those who have been "cooled out" actually internalize failure? Are some student aspirations "heated up" at the community college?

In addition to questions of the type raised above, most of which lend themselves to quantitative analysis, I would also like to make a plea for ethnographic and historical studies. In the quarter-century since Clark's (1960) classic study of a California community college, to my knowledge only three major ethnographic studies have appeared: London's (1978) study of a white, working-class institution, Richardson and others' (1983) study of a heterogeneous, but predominantly white urban community college, and Weis's (1985) study of a black urban institution. Each of these studies told us a great deal about the two-year college that statistical analyses cannot, but more such studies—especially of suburban and small-town community colleges—are needed.

The historical scholarship on community colleges is, if anything, even thinner than the ethnographic literature; there are simply no works available comparable to Veysey (1965) or Rudolph (1962, 1977). Yet first-rate works of historical scholarship are essential if we are to have the perspective to enable us to understand how we have arrived where we are today.

The Future of the Transfer Function. In 1972, I wrote that "the question of whether community colleges should become predominantly vocational institutions may well be the most crucial policy issue facing the two-year institutions in the years ahead" (Karabel, 1972, p. 557). The intervening fourteen years of history have answered that question in the affirmative, but other choices remain to be made. Foremost among them is the fate of the very programs that brought the junior college into being: the liberal arts programs that offered a curriculum parallel to that of the first two years of the university. These programs, historically at the very heart of the two-year college's sense of institutional identity and mission, are in danger of effectively disappearing at many community colleges.

For the working-class and minority students who have flocked to the two-year college in search of the same kinds of opportunities for upward mobility that previous first generations of college students had, much is at stake here. To be sure, in the past the community college has more often been a "revolving door" than a pathway through the portals of four-year colleges and universities—a point that I and other "revisionist" scholars have insisted on in the past and do not wish to retract now. Yet for some students, although never many, the community college was a bridge, connecting those who would otherwise have been excluded to the world of higher education. In a society in which professional and managerial jobs are increasingly monopolized by college graduates, we should know clearly what a weakening of linkages with four-year colleges really means: a cutting off of opportunities for long-range upward mobility for those students, already disproportionately lacking in cultural and economic resources, who are enrolled in higher education's bottom track.

The trend toward an increasingly vocationalized community college—one that is more and more cut off from the mainstream of higher education—is, however, finally meeting with resistance. Stimulated perhaps by the sudden decrease in enrollments that began in 1983 and has since accelerated, community colleges have begun to worry about their declining transfer rates. A variety of factors seem to have been involved in the revival of interest in academic transfer programs—among them, pressure from state legislators concerned about how taxpayer dollars are being spent, new programs funded by foundations concerned about the growing ghettoization of minority youth, and initiatives from student-starved four-year colleges suddenly eager to admit transfers. Above all, however, community colleges have finally begun to remember that historically their link to the rest of higher education has distinguished them from mere trade schools and given them broad public legitimacy and support. If they are to prosper in the future—and if the public is to accord them a level of support commensurate with the formidable tasks they face—they must never again forget this.

References

Alba, R. D., and Lavin, D. E. "Community Colleges and Tracking in Higher Education." *Sociology of Education*, 1981, *54*, 223-247.
Anderson, K. "Post-High School Experience and College Attrition." *Sociology of Education*, 1981, *54*, 1-15.
Astin, A. W. *Minorities in American Higher Education: Recent Trends, Current Prospects, and Recommendations.* San Francisco: Jossey-Bass, 1982.
Astin, A. W., and others. *The American Freshman: National Norms for Fall 1984.* Los Angeles: UCLA Higher Education Research Institute, 1984.
Bourdieu, P. "Cultural Reproduction and Social Reproduction." In J. Karabel and A. H. Halsey (Eds.), *Power and Ideology in Education.* New York: Oxford University Press, 1977.
Bowles, S., and Gintis, H. *Schooling in Capitalist America.* New York: Basic Books, 1976.
Breneman, D. W., and Nelson, S. E. *Financing Community Colleges: An Economic Perspective.* Washington, D.C.: Brookings Institution, 1981.
Brint, S., and Karabel, J. *The Transformation of the Community College.* New York: Oxford University Press, in preparation.
California Postsecondary Education Commission. *Update of Community College Transfer Student Statistics.* Sacramento: California Postsecondary Education Commission, 1984.
Center for the Study of Community Colleges. *Transfer Education in American Community Colleges.* Report to the Ford Foundation. Los Angeles: Center for the Study of Community Colleges, 1985. 313 pp. (ED 255 250)
Chronicle of Higher Education, January 23, 1985, p. 22.
Clark, B. *The Open-Door College: A Case Study.* New York: McGraw-Hill, 1960.
Clark, B. R. "The 'Cooling Out' Function Revisited." In G. B. Vaughan (Ed.), *Questioning the Community College Role.* New Directions for Community Colleges, no. 32. San Francisco: Jossey-Bass, 1980.
Cohen, A. M. "Counting the Transfer Students." *Junior College Resource Review.* Los Angeles: ERIC Clearinghouse for Junior Colleges, 1979. 6 pp. (ED 160 145)
Cohen, A. M. "The Community College in the American Educational System." Paper prepared for the Study Group on the Condition of Excellence in American Education, February 24, 1984.
Cohen, A. M., and Brawer, F. B. *The American Community College.* San Francisco: Jossey-Bass, 1982.
Collins, R. "Functional and Conflict Theories of Educational Stratification." *American Sociological Review*, 1971, *36*, 1002-1019.
Collins, R. *The Credential Society.* New York: Academic Press, 1979.
Dougherty, K. "The Effects of Community Colleges: Aid or Hindrance to Socioeconomic Attainments." Paper presented at the annual meeting of the American Educational Research Association, 1986a.
Dougherty, K. "The Politics of Community College Expansion: Beyond the Functionalist and Class Reproduction Theories." Unpublished paper, Department of Sociology, Manhattanville College, 1986b.
Freeman, R. *The Overeducated American.* New York: Academic Press, 1976.
Friedlander, J. "An ERIC Review: Why Is Transfer Education Declining?" *Community College Review*, 1980, *54*, 59-66.
Grubb, N. "The Bandwagon Once More: Vocational Preparation for High-Tech Occupations." *Harvard Educational Review*, 1984, *54*, 429-451.

Grubb, W. N., and Lazerson, M. "Rally Round the Workplace: Continuities and Fallacies in Career Education." *Harvard Educational Review*, 1975, *45*, 452-474.
Jencks, C., and others. *Who Gets Ahead?* New York: Basic Books, 1979.
Karabel, J. "Community Colleges and Social Stratification." *Harvard Educational Review*, 1972, *42*, 521-562.
Karabel, J. "Protecting the Portals: Class and the Community College." *Social Policy*, 1974, *5*, 12-18.
Karabel, J. "The Politics of Structural Change in American Higher Education: The Case of Open Admissions at the City University of New York." In H. Hermanns and others (Eds.), *The Compleat University: Break from Tradition in Three Countries*. Cambridge: Schenkman, 1983.
Karabel, J. "Status-Group Struggle, Organizational Interests, and the Limits of Institutional Autonomy: The Transformation of Harvard, Yale, and Princeton, 1918-1940." *Theory and Society*, 1984, *13*, 1-40.
Lombardi, J. "The Decline of Transfer Education." Unpublished paper, ERIC Clearinghouse for Junior Colleges, Los Angeles, 1979.
London, H. B. *The Culture of a Community College*. New York: Praeger, 1978.
McCartan, A. M. "The Community College Mission: Present Challenges and Future Visions." *Journal of Higher Education*, 1983, *54* (6), 676-691.
Monk-Turner, E. "Sex, Educational Differentiation, and Occupational Status: Analyzing Occupational Differences for Community and Four-Year College Entrants." *Sociological Quarterly*, 1983, *24*, 393-404.
National Center for Educational Statistics. *The Condition of Education 1985: A Statistical Report*. Washington, D.C.: U.S. Government Printing Office, 1985.
Olivas, M. A. *The Dilemma of Access: Minorities in Two-Year Colleges*. Washington, D.C.: Howard University, 1979.
Oromaner, M. "Insiders, Outsiders, and the Community College: A Sociology of Knowledge Perspective." Unpublished paper, Hudson County (New Jersey) Community College, 1983.
Pincus, F. "Tracking in Community Colleges." *The Insurgent Sociologist*, 1974, *4* (3), 17-35.
Pincus, F. "The False Promises of Community Colleges." *Harvard Educational Review*, 1980, *50*, 332-361.
Richardson, R. C., Jr., Fisk, E. C., and Okun, M. A. *Literacy in the Open-Access College*. San Francisco: Jossey-Bass, 1983.
Riesman, D. *On Higher Education: The Academic Enterprise in an Era of Rising Student Consumerism*. San Francisco: Jossey-Bass, 1981.
Rudolph, F. *The American College and University*. New York: Vintage, 1962.
Rudolph, F. *Curriculum: A History of the American Undergraduate Course of Study Since 1636*. San Francisco: Jossey-Bass, 1977.
Rumberger, R. W. *Overeducation in the U.S. Labor Market*. New York: Praeger, 1981.
Templin, R. G., and Shearon, R. W. "Curriculum Tracking and Social Inequality in the Community College." In G. B. Vaughan (Ed.), *Questioning the Community College Role*. New Directions for Community Colleges, no. 32. San Francisco: Jossey-Bass, 1980.
Tinto, V. "The Distribution Effects of Public Junior College Availability." *Research in Higher Education*, 1975, *3*, 261-274.
Velez, W. "Finishing College: The Effects of College Type." *Sociology of Education*, 1985, *58* (3), 191-200.
Veysey, L. *The Emergence of the American University*. Chicago: The University of Chicago Press, 1965.

Weis, L. *Between Two Worlds: Black Students in an Urban Community College.* Boston: Routledge & Kegan Paul, 1985.

Wilms, W. W. *Public and Proprietary Vocational Training: A Study of Effectiveness.* Berkeley, Calif.: Center for Research and Development in Higher Education, 1974.

Wilms, W., and Hansell, S. "The Dubious Promise of Post-Secondary Vocational Education: Its Payoff to Dropouts and Graduates in the U.S.A." *International Journal of Educational Development,* 1982, *2,* 43–59.

Zwerling, L. S. *Second Best.* New York: McGraw-Hill, 1976.

Jerome Karabel is associate professor of sociology at the University of California, Berkeley, and a senior editor of Theory and Society. *He is co-editor (with A. H. Halsey) of* Power and Ideology in Education *(Oxford University Press, 1977) and is currently at work with Stephen Brint on a book, to be published by Oxford University Press, on the transformation of the community college.*

The community college still represents the first two years of college for millions, but fewer than ever are transferring to four-year colleges.

The Devaluation of Transfer: Current Explanations and Possible Causes

Alison Bernstein

Twenty years ago, in their landmark study of community college transfer students, Knoell and Medsker (1965) wrote: "Junior colleges have made a fine record in preparing students to transfer to a very diverse group of four-year colleges and universities, but improvement in the record is still possible." The generally positive outcome of the study was based on the story of what happened to 7,000 junior college students who transferred in 1960 to forty-three four-year colleges and universities in ten states. Three years after transferring, 62 percent of the students were granted their baccalaureate degrees; another 9 percent were still enrolled at the beginning of the fourth year. Knoell and Medsker estimated that eventually at least 75 percent of the original group would receive their degrees.

The figure of 75 percent is particularly interesting because it also represents the percentage of full-time urban community college students who repeatedly indicate that they plan to earn a baccalaureate degree (Astin and others, 1982). The Knoell and Medsker study concentrated on students who had already transferred from two-year to four-year institutions, negotiating the transition from one collegiate environment to another. The latter survey involved students who are still enrolled in a community college. Unfortunately, if current rates predict trends, fewer than 15 percent of these students will transfer to senior colleges and complete their bachelor's degrees three years later.

Declining Transfer Rates

Some critics of community colleges have argued that community colleges were deliberately designed to "cool out" or derail students who aspired to complete the baccalaureate degree (Clark, 1960; Karabel, 1972; Zwerling, 1976). This institutional function, however, has seldom worked perfectly. Community college students have historically used community colleges to enhance their educational mobility. While the flow from two- to four-year colleges has never been a flood, what once was a steady stream has recently been reduced in some institutions to little more than a trickle. In California, where over a million students are enrolled in community colleges, the number who transferred to the University of California (UC) in 1973 was 8,193; by 1984, the overall number was 5,257, or a decline of approximately 40 percent. The comparable figures for the California State University (CSU) system are somewhat more encouraging: approximately 30,000 community college students, or 3 percent of the total community college enrollment, transferred into CSU in 1984. As in the UC example, the number who have transferred to CSU is down over 5,000 from a high of 35,537 in 1975 (California Postsecondary Education Commission, 1985).

The California phenomenon of declining transfer rates mirrors the experiences of other states. If one looks at the population of associate degree recipients coming from the State University system of New York (SUNY) in what have been traditionally called transfer or "university parallel" programs (A.A. and A.A.S. degree recipients only), the percentage of transfers has also decreased. In 1975-1976, SUNY's two-year colleges enrolled 3,415 transfers with these degrees. By 1982-1983, 9,790 A.A. or A.A.S. degrees were granted, but transfers with these degrees had dropped to 2,146. In other words, the number of "university parallel" degree recipients had dropped by 2.7 percent, but the number of transfers to senior institutions with these degrees had dropped by 37 percent (Bader-Borel, 1985). Lombardi (1979) compiled statistics on transfer rates in several states and found similar discouraging patterns: In Florida, the number of transfers declined from 9.9 percent of the community college enrollment to 7.4 percent in the period from 1973 to 1978; in Washington, the comparable figures were 3.3 percent in 1973 to 2.1 percent in 1978. Kintzer and Wattenbarger (1985) updated Lombardi's statistics and found overall declines in six of nine states that enroll significant numbers of community college students—California, Florida, Washington, New Jersey, North Carolina, and Maryland. Given the small number of states collecting transfer statistics and the lack of uniformity regarding the definition of a transfer student, we do not have solid national longitudinal data regarding the flow of students from two- to four-year colleges. Until national statistics become available, it is safe to conclude that fewer than 5 percent of full- and part-time community college students transfer with junior status to colleges and universities (Cohen and Brawer, 1982).

The decline in transfer rates of community college students is even more significant, since this sector of higher education remains the crucial point of access for millions of low-income and minority students wishing to pursue higher education. More than half of all blacks attending college are in two-year institutions. In California, 90 percent of all full- and part-time Chicano students in higher education attend community colleges (California Postsecondary Education Commission, 1985). While nationally only 27 percent of whites who attend college on a full-time basis enroll in community colleges, these institutions enroll 37 percent of blacks and 45 percent of Hispanic full-time students. In other words, they serve greater proportions of minority students than they do students from any other single sector. These colleges have also become the main entry points to higher education for migrants from Puerto Rico and for immigrant populations—Cubans in Florida, Mexican-Americans in the Southwest, and Asian-Americans on the Pacific coast. In addition to minorities, community colleges enroll millions of working men and women for whom this is the last opportunity for a college-level education. For a variety of reasons (including money, academic preparation, geography, and comfort), 49 percent of all undergraduates begin the journey through American higher education in community colleges (Warren, 1985, p. 54).

Given this democratic context, community colleges must understand the importance of their mission as collegiate institutions and not view themselves simply as educational sites offering whatever formal courses of instruction individuals, local communities, or industries wish to support. Central to the community college's collegiate mission is its role in facilitating the transfer of students from one level of higher education to another, yet no function has been more misunderstood or recently neglected by community college administrators and faculty.

This chapter discusses the decline of transfer rates in community colleges, by highlighting two themes: (1) the inadequacy of conventional explanations for the decline in transfer and (2) more likely, underlying policies and practices that affect transfer.

The Student-Centered Explanation

Few community college administrators and faculty dispute the fact that for over a decade the flow of community college students into baccalaureate degree–granting institutions has been slowing down. They and others have offered several explanations for this decline. Some explanations are more defensive than others, but most lack hard statistical evidence. The most commonly held reason given for the decline in transfer has been the student-centered explanation. Students are not moving through two-year colleges in the same numbers as they once did because they are not as interested in transfer as they once were. This explanation takes responsibility for performing the transfer function from the institution and places it squarely on the students. Parnell (1985) has argued that for the average student in a community college, a baccalaureate degree is not the goal: "We must constantly remind ourselves that the majority of our population will never earn a baccalaureate degree." He carefully chooses his terms and tenses; if current patterns continue, not even a third, let alone a majority, of the community college population will ever complete the B.A. degree. Parnell, however, leaves a crucial variable out of his analysis, namely, student aspiration. If this variable is taken into account, it will be seen that over half of all community college students, and even up to 75 percent, regularly indicate that they aspire to complete the baccalaureate. This does not mean that all these students have the academic preparation needed to succeed in upper-division studies. It does signify that Parnell's "neglected majority" has a compelling interest in baccalaureate-level learning. That their transfer and degree-completion rates do not reflect their aspirations suggests that the student-centered explanation is not sufficient.

In a review of enrollment trends, Friedlander (1980) offers several specific variations on this student-centered explanation. After noting that typically fewer than 10 percent of community college students actually transfer, Friedlander suggests that this rate could be attributed to shifting student interests, from academic to occupational courses; the growing proportion of community college students who linger and eventually drop out of remedial courses; and the increasing number of students who take a disjointed course of study because they attend college part-time. These explanations are based on data drawn from Friedlander's demographic observations on community colleges and provide important perspectives on the differences between collegiate life at community colleges and at more traditional, residential colleges.

They do not, however, sufficiently distinguish community college students from open-admissions, public urban university students. In fact, the enrollment trends Friedlander describes can be seen at Cuyahoga Community College (Tri-C), at Cleveland State University, at Sacramento City College, and at California State University at Sacramento. All these institutions enroll students who are increasingly part-timers, occupationally minded, and in need of remediation. Nevertheless, there is a greater likelihood that a student will finish a baccalaureate degree at Cleveland State if she began there than if she enrolled first at Tri-C and planned to transfer. In other words, Friedlander's observations do not adequately contrast urban community college students with their four-year urban public college counterparts to demonstrate that the characteristics of community college students account for low transfer and baccalaureate completion rates. Blaming the decline in transfer on student characteristics, therefore, is an inadequate response.

After examining some other characteristics of current community college students who transfer, one discovers other factors suggesting that Friedlander's explanations are not especially useful. For example, of those students who are transferring, an increasing majority are coming from occupational and "terminal" A.A.S. degree programs, as opposed to university-parallel programs. Where conventional wisdom once assumed that the so-called vocational courses of study would lead students away from the baccalaureate degree, the reverse appears to be the case. A majority of colleges are reporting an increase in the percentage of A.A.S. degree completions, in spite of an overall decline in the absolute number of associate degrees awarded. Moreover, the A.A.S. graduates appear more likely to transfer to senior colleges and pursue their baccalaureates. Thus, the vocational or occupational orientation of these students does not appear to be a disincentive to transfer, as Friedlander suggests. Also, these students are as likely as "transfer track" students to enroll on a part-time basis and need remedial courses to make up for deficiencies in writing and reading.

Another dimension of the problem of declining transfer rates, which is frequently misunderstood in the student-centered explanation, refers to the academic preparation of community college students. In two- as well as four-year institutions, there has been an increase in the amount of remedial work students are required to take before proceeding to appropriate college-level courses. A recent national report, for example, indicates that "82 percent of colleges and universities offered at least one remedial course in mathematics, reading, or writing in 1983-1984" (Wright, 1985). This increase in remediation, most apparent in two-year colleges, public institutions, and those with open admissions, comes at a time when data about community college students suggest that the academic preparation of these students has been improving. Warren (1985) notes, for example, that "about half of the entering full-time community college students in 1970 reported that they had been in the top half of their high school classes. By 1982, that proportion had grown to three-fourths" (p. 60). Additionally, approximately 20 percent of high school graduates in the top quarter of their classes currently enroll in community colleges, thus providing an academically able cohort likely to be interested in transfer.

It is true that community college students are generally less well prepared than students in four-year institutions, but there is still a growing, above-average pool of high school graduates who are enrolling in community colleges because of low cost and geographical proximity. Most of these students, regardless of their vocational interests, aspire to complete baccalaureate degrees. The recent decline in overall transfer rates, however, suggests that these more able students appear to be a population that is not taken seriously by community college faculty and administrators. This neglect is particularly troubling in urban community colleges, which largely serve minority students. In short, recent data regarding the academic characteristics of community college students offer evidence that declines in transfer rates cannot be attributed solely to students' inadequate preparation.

Institutionally Oriented Explanations

If the conventional, student-oriented explanations for the decline in transfer leave as many questions as they purportedly answer, there may be other, more institutionally-oriented explanations that point to underlying structural causes. Recent analyses by Richardson (1985) and Lavin and others (1984) suggest that the institutional climate of community colleges may overtly or more subtly undermine their students' baccalaureate aspirations. This approach argues that even if most community colleges do not subsribe to a "cooling out" philosophy, many may in practice perform a "cooling out" function. While not attempting to place value judgments on either sector, Richardson argues that community colleges and universities represent different academic cultures. For example, community college faculty base their standards of how a student performs on comparisons with the performance of others taking the same class. In contrast, university faculty grade students by measuring them against a standard that does not change with variations in preparation or aptitude of those enrolled in the courses. This difference between norm-referenced and criterion-referenced assessment reflect one gap between the values of the community college and those of the four-year institution. The latter is warm, nurturing, and rewards self-exploration as the goal of education; the former emphasizes achievement and mastery, not over self but over curriculum, and through the development of specific cognitive skills. Given the dichotomies that can emerge from these two value systems, it is likely that students who wish to transfer from one environment to another face a difficult journey. Success in adapting to the culture of a community college may negatively affect a student's chances of persisting at the upper-division level.

The institutional environment of community colleges can be better understood if one looks to specific academic practices. In general, four-year college faculty are more likely to assign readings and use written work as the basis of grading. Among the faculty surveyed in one study (Center for the Study of Community Colleges, 1985), 52 percent indicated that one-fourth or more of a student's final grade is based on performance in quick-score objective tests. In contrast, only 27 percent of the faculty indicated essay tests as representing more than one-fourth of a student's final grade. Surveys of students in the same community colleges reinforced the faculty's own reports. For the majority of students in transfer classes, the average number of written assignments was less than five. Another indicator of the differences in academic climates was related specifically to faculty roles and responsibilities. A majority (67 percent) of faculty teaching transfer-oriented courses did not have information on student transfer aspirations; 81 percent had no information about students' performance on basic-skills tests; 80 percent knew nothing of students' employment status. Additionally, only a small fraction of the faculty reported frequent meetings with students to discuss transfer procedures and opportunities. The limited picture of faculty involvement in the transfer function is matched by faculty attitudes toward transfer:

> Despite agreement from more than half of the faculty sample that students will have a greater sense of accomplishment if they earn the baccalaureate degree, less than one-fifth of the respondents . . . agreed that the primary function of the community college should be that of preparing students for transfer to senior institutions. Additionally, only 17 percent agreed that transfer education should be the college's most important function. . . . Evidently, the majority of the faculty shares the philosophy espoused by advocates of the community college movement—a philosophy grounded on the belief that the character of the colleges precludes programmatic priorities, as well as measures of effectiveness based on graduation and transfer rates [Center for the Study of Community Colleges, 1985, p. 90].

If faculty who teach the transfer curriculum do not believe in the primacy of this function, it is also unlikely that the institution will take it seriously.

Nevertheless, it may also be true that faculty are simply reflecting the administration's priorities. As Richardson (1985) and Seidman (1985) have noted, community college administrators often have more influence on curriculum and instruction than university administrators do. While the devaluation of transfer may occur institutionally, the behaviors and expectations that faculty convey to students nevertheless ultimately carry the greatest potential for negative impact. If faculty expectations for students are low, and if faculty do not encourage students to achieve higher levels of mastery, then transfer aspirants can easily become community college dropouts. Clearly, more research and analysis is needed to determine what role faculty attitudes and academic environmental factors play in the devaluation of the transfer function. We do know, however, that not all community colleges have the same transfer rates; some are significantly better than others, even when we control for the students' socioeconomic backgrounds and levels of previous preparation (Alba and Lavin, 1981).

One extrainstitutional factor not previously mentioned—funding—may also negatively affect the transfer function. If a community college is funded through a formula that rewards "seat-time" (that is, course credit enrollments on a single day during the semester), there is no incentive for the institution to program sequenced educational offerings or a university-parallel curriculum. It probably does not pay institutionally to maintain upper-level (sophomore) courses, which typically enroll fewer students but nevertheless fulfill transfer requirements. An important index of the value an institution places on successfully performing the transfer function may be the number of sophomore-level courses regularly offered, regardless of the number of students electing them. Another measure of the community college's attention to transfer may be the number of courses that have prerequisites. Prerequisites indicate that the faculty and administration are taking care to move students through a sequenced and increasingly rigorous curriculum.

Finally, some attention should be paid to interinstitutional factors. Deegan and others (1985) have argued that there has been a major breakdown in articulation among segments of higher education: "Responsibility for such neglect is so widespread that problems with the transfer function should not be placed solely at the door of the community colleges." Despite a certain defensiveness, this explanation offers some encouragement that one era, when community college advocates viewed their institutions as "above and beyond" the rest of traditional, elitist higher education, is over. That kind of uncritical self-promotion provided a convenient excuse for the other collegiate segments to disregard community colleges as "below and beside" the point. Improving transfer rates, and reversing the decline in the numbers of community college students (especially minority students) who complete baccalaureate degrees, are joint responsibilities of two- and four-year institutions. Better and more programmatic articulation between and within systems can have a positive effect on transfer. It must be added, however, that there is no evidence to suggest that simple agreements between institutions result in higher transfer rates. These educational "treaties" may not have much effect on factors that govern teaching and learning. When the time comes to evaluate credits, students may find that much of their previous work will not be accepted for credit toward the major or distribution requirements. In other words, the articulation agreements may not be worth the paper on which they were written.

Many Students Transfer

In reviewing explanations for the decline of transfer in contemporary community colleges, this chapter has naturally focused on the negative: on the discontinuities between two- and four-year institutions and on factors (other than student characteristics) that may account for the devaluation of transfer as a primary community college function. Despite the problems enumerated, however, many community college students have remarkable persistence. In the City University of New York, for example, on-time graduation rates for community college students are exceedingly low. "Most of the A.A. graduates received their degrees three, four, and even five years after entry" (Lavin and others, 1984, p. 9). Unfortunately, the CUNY study does not follow up on transfer and baccalaureate completion rates. Nevertheless, after eleven years 45 percent of regular community college students who entered CUNY in 1970, and 28 percent of the less well-prepared open-admissions students, completed their community college studies. Thus, CUNY may have a long-term transfer and baccalaureate-completion rate that exceeds current national averages. Likewise, Pascarella and others (1985) offered findings from a national representative sample showing that 53 percent of community college students who expressed an interest in achieving the baccalaureate actually did so over a nine-year period. These studies offer convincing evidence that community college students not only aspire to complete their baccalaureate degrees but are also prepared to spend a considerable amount of time doing so. The goal for community and four-year colleges is to make that journey as efficient, educationally rewarding, and challenging as possible.

References

Alba, R., and Lavin, D. E. "Community Colleges and Tracking in Higher Education." *Sociology of Education,* 1981, *54,* 223-237.

Astin, A. W., Hemond, M. K., and Richardson, G. T. *The American Freshman: National Norms for 1982.* Los Angeles: University of California, 1982.

Bader-Borel, P. (Ed). *Compilation of Statistical Data Concerning the Community Colleges of the State University of New York, 1983-84.* Albany: Office for Community Colleges, Office of Finance and Business, and Office of Institutional Research and Planning, State University of New York, 1984. 368 pp. (ED 253 280)

California Postsecondary Education Commission. *Update of Community College Transfer Student Statistics, 1984: Commission Report 85-21.* Sacramento, Calif.: California Postsecondary Education Commission, 1985, 48 pp. (ED 256 399)

Center for the Study of Community Colleges. *Transfer Education in American Community Colleges.* Los Angeles: Center for the Study of Community Colleges, 1985. 313 pp. (ED 255 250)

Clark, B. "The Cooling-Out Function of Higher Education." *American Journal of Sociology,* 1960, *65,* 569-576.

Cohen, A. M., and Brawer, F. B. *The American Community College.* San Francisco: Jossey-Bass, 1982.

Deegan, W. L., Tillery, D., and Associates. *Renewing the American Community College: Priorities and Strategies for Effective Leadership.* San Francisco: Jossey-Bass, 1985.

Friedlander, J. "An ERIC Review: Why Is Transfer Education Declining?" *Community College Review*, 1980, *8* (2), 59-66.

Karabel, J. "Community Colleges and Social Stratification: Submerged Class Conflict in American Higher Education." *Harvard Education Review*, 1972, *42* (4), 521-562.

Kintzer, F. C., and Wattenbarger, J. L. *The Articulation/Transfer Phenomenon: Patterns and Directions.* Washington, D.C.: The American Association of Community and Junior Colleges, 1985.

Knoell, D. M., and Medsker, L. *From Junior to Senior College.* Washington, D.C.: American Council on Education, 1965.

Lavin, D. E., Murtha, J., and Kaufman, B. "Long-Term Graduation Rates of Students at the City University of New York." New York: City University of New York, 1984.

Lombardi, J. A. *The Decline of Transfer Education, Topical Paper Number 70.* ERIC Clearinghouse for Junior College Information, University of California, 1979. 37 pp. (ED 179 273)

Parnell, D. *The Neglected Majority.* Washington, D.C.: The Community College Press, 1985.

Pascarella, E. T., Smart, J. C., and Ethington, C. A. "Long-Term Persistence of Two-Year College Students." Paper presented at the Association for the Study of Higher Education, 1985.

Richardson, R. C. Keynote Speech at the CUNY Articulation Conference, City University of New York, 1985.

Seidman, E. *In Their Own Words: Perspectives on Improving Teaching and Educational Quality in Community Colleges.* San Francisco: Jossey-Bass, 1985.

Warren, J. "The Changing Characteristics of Community College Students." In W. L. Deegan and D. Tillery (Eds.), *Renewing the American Community College: Priorities and Strategies for Effective Leadership.* San Francisco: Jossey-Bass, 1985.

Wright, D. A. *Many College Freshmen Take Remedial Courses.* Washington, D.C.: National Center for Education Statistics, 1985. 16 pp. (ED 262 742)

Zwerling, L. S. *Second Best: The Crisis of the Community College.* New York: McGraw-Hill, 1976.

Alison Bernstein is a historian who works as a program officer at the Ford Foundation.

Vocational education does not serve the interests of poor and minority students who desire economic security and upward mobility.

Vocational Education: More False Promises

Fred L. Pincus

Terminal vocational education has been a central part of the community college mission for over fifty years, and it also has been a source of controversy. Supporters have emphasized the way in which postsecondary vocational education has served the business community and the larger society by training skilled workers. In addition, they have argued that these programs are avenues of upward mobility for low-income and minority students, who are not well served by the traditional college curriculum. More recently, two-year vocational programs have been described as an important weapon in the trade war between the United States and its capitalist rivals.

Community college critics acknowledge that vocational education benefits the business community, but they reject the argument that these programs benefit low-income and minority students. Critics argue that while community colleges are the lowest track in a stratified system of higher education, terminal vocational programs are the lowest track in the two-year colleges. Since students at the bottom of the economic ladder are overrepresented in terminal vocational programs, critics argue, they are deprived of the greater intellectual and economic benefits that come from getting a bachelor's degree. Consequently, community colleges help to reproduce the race and economic inequalities that exist in the larger society.

In the midst of this controversy, one thing is clear—the public community colleges are predominantly vocational training institutions. In the 1980s, more than two-thirds of degree-seeking students are enrolled in vocational programs, and 71 percent of all associate degrees and certificates were awarded in vocational areas. In 1970, only 25 percent of enrollment and 45 percent of degrees were vocational.

Empirical Evidence

In spite of these dramatic trends, little is known about the economic benefits of vocational programs to the students. Since most community college proponents tend to support vocational programs by pointing to a few successful graduates, I tried to review the empirical evidence that existed in the late 1970s (Pincus, 1980). The main findings did not provide strong support for the dramatic increase in postsecondary vocational programs.

Jobs. Over half of former vocational students got the jobs for which they were trained, although there were often dramatic differences from one program to another. Students who completed vocational programs did not necessarily have advantages over the noncompleters in terms of job placement.

Unemployment. Former vocational students were less likely to be unemployed than high school graduates who did not attend college. At best, their unemployment rates were the same as the rates of college graduates, but they were probably higher. Program completers had lower unemployment rates than noncompleters.

Income. Former vocational students had higher incomes than high school graduates but lower incomes than college graduates. Men had dramatically higher incomes than women. Surprisingly, students who failed to complete vocational programs tended to have higher incomes than program completers.

In the more than five years since this article was published, several other studies have come to similar conclusions. Breneman and Nelson (1981) analyzed the National Longitudinal Study of 1972 high school graduates. They found that although attending community colleges increased former students' chances of being employed, relative to those who attended four-year colleges, it decreased their occupational status and had no effect on wages. They concluded: "Since occupational status is generally considered to be highly correlated with adult earnings, the positive relationship between attending a university and occupational status bodes ill for future earnings for students choosing a community college instead of a university right after high school" (p. 72). Unfortunately, they did not examine the effects of enrolling in a vocational program, as compared with a transfer program.

A study of the 1980 graduates of Maryland community colleges does provide some evidence on this issue (Maryland State Board for Community Colleges, 1983). The 1981 mean income of transfer graduates was $14,746. This was $1,139 lower than the incomes of data-processing graduates and $1,558 lower than the incomes of mechanical and engineering graduates. In contrast, the mean income of transfer graduates was between $740 and $4,057 higher than that of the graduates of four other vocational programs—public service business and commerce, health, and natural sciences. In other words, transfer graduates had salaries that were comparable to the average salaries of all vocational graduates.

Wilms (1980) did a sophisticated follow-up study of the 1973 entrants to six vocational programs in four metropolitan areas across the country. For students in higher-status occupational programs (accounting, computer programming, and electronic technology), the type of first job a student obtained after leaving the college had no relationship to whether the students had completed the program. Even more important, while only a minority of men got technical or managerial-level jobs, not a single woman in these programs got such a high-level job.

The findings for students enrolled in the predominantly female, lower-status programs (secretary, dental assistant, cosmetology) was quite different. Program completion did increase the likelihood of getting a job for which the student was trained, and a majority of the completers did get these jobs.

Wilms also looked at the earnings of former vocational students. The results of a regression analysis showed that student-background variables were better predictors of earnings than school variables. Males and older people tended to have the highest incomes. Race and socioeconomic status were also related to earnings, but in a weaker and less consistent way. Program completion and even type of program were irrelevant in determining the earnings of former students.

All in all, the empirical studies of former vocational education students do not provide much support to the argument that terminal programs in community colleges provide avenues to decent jobs and upward mobility. Clearly, a student would be better off completing a bachelor's degree at a four-year college. At best, vocational students are better off than high school graduates with no postsecondary education. In a recent paper on a research agenda for community colleges, Richardson (1985) argues: "Even though community college administrators have been extremely critical of the studies by Pincus . . . and Wilms . . . , there have not been comparable studies in most states to provide better information" (p. 7).

Community college supporters often respond by saying that these conclusions are not warranted. First, they argue that the transfer-terminal distinction is obsolete, since many technical students actually transfer to four-year colleges, and many liberal arts students do not. Second, supporters say that students in the upper-level vocational programs, such as computer programming and electronics, are more academically capable than many students in transfer programs and may earn higher salaries than many students with liberal arts bachelor's degrees. Consequently, larger numbers of reverse-transfer students are moving from four-year to two-year colleges to take advantage of these programs. Finally, say supporters, in evaluating the effectiveness of vocational education it is necessary to take student goals into account. Students who do not plan to transfer or to complete vocational programs should not be called dropouts.

If evaluations took these factors into account, say supporters, vocational education would be shown to be an effective program that helps students achieve their educational and occupational goals. Presumably, the supporters also believe that these "more accurate" evaluations would undermine the argument that vocational education helps to reproduce social inequality based on race, class, and sex.

A sophisticated longitudinal study of students who entered California community colleges in 1978 incorporates many of these principles, and I would like to examine some of the findings (Sheldon, 1982). Students were placed into different "prototypes" on the basis of their stated goals, their academic skills, their majors, and their patterns of enrollment and course completion.

Given these criteria, students who said they wanted to transfer were placed into one of four categories. Full-time (1) and part-time (2) transfer students were taking a sequence of courses that could lead to the associate degree and to transfer. Technical transfer students (3) majored in one of the higher-status technical programs, with the intention of transferring, and were taking courses in sequence. The undisciplined transfer students (4) lacked "either the academic skills to complete their work or the self-discipline to follow through on their studies and homework" (Sheldon, 1982, pp. 1-30).

Vocational students were also placed into one of four categories. Program completers (1) aspired to complete an entire program of study. Job seekers (2) wanted to take courses until they found jobs. Job upgraders (3) wanted a few courses to get raises or promotions in their current jobs. Career changers (4) wanted to take a few courses so they could move from one job to another. The career changers and the job upgraders were considerably older than the other two groups of vocational students and had more experience in the labor market.

These prototypes do make a difference when one examines the educational and economic outcomes of students two and one-half years after they entered. For example, although the overall transfer rate is low, saying that only 9.5 percent of all students transferred to four-year colleges is somewhat misleading. Among transfer students, full-time students were the most likely to transfer (32.1 percent) while the undisciplined students were the least likely (7.5 percent). Only 3.2 percent of the vocational students had transferred.

In contrast, the California data clearly show that minority students are most likely to be found in the least desirable prototypes. Among the undisciplined transfer students, for example, blacks and Hispanics are overrepresented, while whites are underrepresented. The opposite is true for the full-time transfer students. Students who say that they are financially disadvantaged are also overrepresented among the undisciplined students and underrepresented among the full-time students. Women are underrepresented in all four categories.

Among the vocational students, the job seekers are the worst off, since they are looking for jobs but not taking any clear sequence of courses. They had the second-lowest hourly salaries upon entering the college and had the lowest salary increases two and one-half years later. Not surprisingly, whites were underrepresented among these students, while blacks, Hispanics, women, and the financially disadvantaged were overrepresented. In contrast, the job upgraders had the highest hourly wages upon entering the college and the highest salary increases two and one-half years later. Whites were overrepresented in this group, blacks were equally represented, and Hispanics, women, and the financially disadvantaged were underrepresented.

These prototypes could help to explain the previous findings that program completion does not necessarily lead to higher earnings. Job upgraders already had jobs and were taking a few courses (an average of thirteen credits) to upgrade themselves. Although only 11 percent completed a program, their hourly income increased by $2.44 (about $0.19 per credit) over two and one-half years. Program completers, in contrast, were taking more courses (an average of forty-five credits) to try to find new jobs. Their initial salaries were 38 percent lower than those of the job upgraders. Although 23 percent of them completed their programs, their salaries increased by only $1.93 (about $0.04 per credit) over two and one-half years. Once again, those who seemed to benefit the most from vocational education were those who were the most privileged when they entered the college.

Income data for transfer students are presented for all four prototypes combined. Their initial salaries were slightly higher than those of the program completers, and their salary increases were somewhat lower. However, since they took fewer credits than program completers, their salaries increased about $0.05 for each credit. This is comparable to the rate of increase for the program completers. Once again, if a student is enrolling in a community college looking for a job, it is not clear that enrolling in a liberal arts transfer program is any worse than trying to complete most vocational programs.

Finally, the California data provide some information about the reverse-transfer phenomenon. There were 13 percent of all students who said that they had attended four-year colleges prior to entering community colleges, and 7 percent said they had bachelor's degrees. However, these students were not evenly distributed across the different prototypes. One-quarter of the career changers were reverse-transfers, as were 19 percent of the job upgraders and 15 percent of the part-time transfers. None of the other prototypes had more than 8 percent of its students as reverse-transfers. One-quarter of leisure-skills students, an additional prototype who take courses for the fun of it, were also reverse-transfers. With the exception of the part-time transfers, the reverse-transfers tend to be in prototypes with higher initial and final salaries and more labor market experience than the majority of community college students have. They tend to use the community college differently from those who are trying to climb the economic ladder.

I discuss the California data in such detail because they tend to support many of the general arguments made by the community college critics, even though the study was conducted by a community college supporter. The least advantaged students tend to be overrepresented in the prototypes that gain the fewest economic benefits from education.

Vocational Education and High Technology

During the past five years, proponents of vocation education have been trying to climb onto the high-tech bandwagon by saying that community colleges can train middle-level workers for rapidly growing, high-skill occupations in the world of computers and electronics. More than half the twenty fastest growing occupations required community college training.

Skeptics have argued that high technology offers too little for too few. The empirical data, based on government projections (Silvestri and others, 1983; Riche and others, 1983) and studies by economists (Rumberger and Levin, 1984) suggest the following conclusions:

1. A small minority of the labor force is presently employed in high-tech *industries,* and this is not expected to change by 1995.

2. Only a minority of workers in these industries are employed in technology-oriented *occupations* that are growing at a rapid rate.

3. Most of the twenty occupations that will add the greatest number of new jobs to the labor force by 1995 require no more than a high school education.

4. Lower-paying jobs are growing at a faster rate than higher-paying jobs.

These findings are consistent with the argument that high technology causes a polarizing effect by creating a small number of high-skilled jobs and a much larger number of low-skill jobs (Pincus, 1983; for an opposing view, see Grubb, 1984).

In terms of community college enrollment and degrees, programs related to high technology would be expected to be small but rapidly growing. Unfortunately, enrollment statistics are not very reliable and consistent over time. The government does, however, keep annual data on the number of subbaccalaureate degrees and certificates granted each year. During the four-year period between 1978-79 and 1981-82, all types of occupational degrees grew at an annual rate of less than 4 percent. Degrees in computer programming, however, increased at an annual rate of 34.5 percent, while degrees for electronics technicians increased at a rate of 19.9 percent (Grubb and Jussaud, 1984).

Taken together, however, computer programming and electronics technology accounted for only 8.8 percent of all occupational degrees in 1981. There were more degrees granted in secretarial science in 1982 than in electronics technology, and more practical (vocational) nurses received degrees than did computer programmers. In other words, community colleges are basically training people for the same types of lower-level jobs that they trained people for fifteen years ago (Grant and Eiden, 1984).

It is also important to understand that many high-technology industries are highly stratified, and that community colleges do not train the most skilled workers. In the field of data processing, systems analysts are the most skilled. Systems programmers are also highly skilled and, like the analysts, tend to have bachelor's or higher degrees. Applications programmers do some of the more routine programming work and are likely to have associate degrees from community colleges. Computer technicians, those who repair the machines, are also likely to have community college training. The bottom rung of the data-processing ladder is filled with lower-skilled operators and data-entry personnel.

The number of systems analysts, computer operators, and technicians is expected to grow rapidly, while the number of data-entry personnel is expected to decline. Here is what the *Occupational Outlook Handbook* has to say about programmers: "The demand for applications programmers will increase, as many more processes once done by hand are automated, but employment is not expected to grow as rapidly as in the past. Improved software, such as utility programs that can be used by other than data-processing personnel, will simplify or eliminate some programming tasks. More systems programmers will be needed to develop and maintain the complex operating programs made necessary by higher-level computer languages, as well as to link or coordinate the output of different computer systems" (Bureau of Labor Statistics, 1982, p. 231; see also Greenbaum, 1976). In other words, community college–trained programmers are likely to face rough times relatively soon, especially as the field becomes glutted, given the high enrollments.

This hierarchy of occupations within data processing also reflects a continuing sex division of labor. Only one-third of the bachelor's degrees in computer science go to women, compared to slightly more than half the subbaccalaureate degrees in computer programming. In other words, fewer women are being trained to be upper-level systems analysts and programmers than are trained to be applications programmers. If Wilms (1980) is correct, many of these women never get jobs as applications programmers when they leave community colleges. Almost two-thirds of those who receive degrees as computer operators, and three-fourths who receive data-entry degrees, are women. The only predominantly male area in data processing at the community college level is computer technology, a relatively well-paying technical job. In other words, the community colleges help to perpetuate a stratified labor force, in which men get the more skilled, higher-paying jobs (Grant and Eiden, 1984).

The issue of skill is also important, in terms of looking at employers' perceptions of vocational education. Most observers assume that employers look to postsecondary vocational education as a source of technically skilled workers, yet Wilms (1984) found that less than one-third of the employers looking for entry-level workers at the professional, technical, managerial, and sales levels preferred applicants with postsecondary vocational training over those with liberal arts educations. In addition, these employers said that technical skills were not the most important attribute that they looked for in an applicant: "In the eyes of most employers, the chief value of an educational credential—especially a postsecondary degree—is to insure that the applicant has good work habits and positive attitudes" (p. 349; also see Crain, 1984). Once again, the importance of specific technical skills for employment in today's competitive labor market seems to be exaggerated.

Contract Training

It is bad enough that community colleges have become so "vocationalized" with respect to degree-credit enrollment. An even more ominous sign is the stampede to get involved in contract training courses for business and industry. In their enthusiasm to seek new sources of revenue and students, community college leaders seem unaware of or unconcerned about the potential danger to their educational institutions.

Most of these contracts involve individual employers who pay colleges to train employees in specific, hands-on skills. Courses typically last from a few hours to a few weeks and are customized to the needs of individual employers. These customized contract training (CCT) courses do not even make a pretense of being well rounded and offering students transferable skills.

In the only national survey of CCT, Deegan and Drisko (1985) found that more than two-thirds of the responding community colleges had signed at least one contract. In contrast to proponents' claims that CCT courses serve business, labor, and other sectors of the community, the authors found that two-thirds of the contracts were signed with business and industry, while fewer than 4 percent were signed with labor unions. The median number of contracts held was eight, and two-thirds of the courses were offered at the job sites. The authors conclude: "A large majority of the respondents expressed the opinion that contract training will be of increasing importance in the future of community colleges" (p. 17).

Typically, proponents argue that everyone benefits from CCT. Employers get low-cost worker training, which increases productivity and profits. Employee-students gain increased skills, which presumably increase their job security and salaries. Colleges get increased revenue, more students, a better-trained faculty, and more state-of-the-art equipment.

Critics see this view as overly simplistic (Pincus, 1985). Corporations, workers, and educators have many conflicting interests, as well as some in common. What is good for General Motors is not necessarily good for everyone else. CCT "makes the firm or the corporation the client and principal beneficiary of the program. Any broader educational needs of the students necessarily are of secondary importance" (Pratzner, 1983, p. 14).

It is clear that business can gain substantial benefits from CCT. Large corporations with substantial in-house training programs can maintain more flexibility and reduce costs by contracting out some of the training. If the state has funds to subsidize this training, so much the better.

Whether workers gain much from CCT remains to be seen. When General Motors uses community colleges to teach dealer technicians (auto mechanics) how to repair the new models, it is doubtful that any salary increases go along with the training. Systematic follow-up studies of employee-students in CCT courses are virtually nonexistent.

Although colleges gain certain resources from CCT, they may have to give up more than they bargain for. The employer, for example, has the main voice in determining the content of courses. This goes far beyond the "advisory role" that employers generally play in shaping the vocational education curriculum. There is always the danger that CCT will drain even more resources from the already weakened liberal arts component of the curriculum. Finally, it is possible that colleges will attempt to "cleanse" faculties of any antibusiness elements in order to secure their new partnerships with the business community.

It is extremely disconcerting that few if any community college leaders discuss these issues. It is possible to argue that all these problems can be avoided by well-informed educators, but one cannot be too optimistic if educators tend to ignore potential problems.

Conclusion

By and large, there is no good evidence that vocational education in community colleges delivers on the promises of secure employment, decent pay, and ample career opportunities. In fact, most of the evidence suggests that while a few relatively privileged workers can make use of community colleges to upgrade their skills, most students would be better advised to get bachelor's degrees, if they can.

This conclusion is consistent with one of the major thrusts of the "excellence" movement of the 1980s. Virtually every major report that has been issued on the state of education during the past few years has emphasized the need for strong liberal arts training, with a special emphasis on basic skills. The "excellence" movement has either ignored vocational education or criticized it for being too narrowly focused (Gross and Gross, 1985).

Predictably, the proponents of community college vocational education have responded defensively. Parnell (1985) expressed concern for "ordinary students" who will not get bachelor's degrees. For these students, Parnell proposes a "2 + 2 tech/prep" associate degree, in coordination with the high schools. Under this plan, students in the eleventh grade could select the tech/prep option. While in high school, they would get training in basic literacy and technical skills, all with an applied focus. In the community college, the students would take more specialized technical courses, which would lead to employment after two years.

If the economic returns of vocational education are as bad as I have suggested in this chapter, then it would do students no good to select the tech/prep option in high school. Tech/prep students would be hurt, since in effect they would be reducing their educational aspirations by the junior year of high school.

At the very least, it is important for community colleges to be more candid with their students. If a student knows all the facts and still wants training to be a dental assistant or a secretary, fine. However, if students were aware of all the facts and the different options that are open to them, they might well select the community college transfer programs in much larger numbers.

Of course, such a development could contribute to the continuing problem of underemployment (sometimes called *overeducation*). For the past fifteen years, policy makers have been concerned that the growth in the number of college graduates is outstripping the number of available college-level jobs. In fact, terminal vocational education has often been proposed as the solution to the problem of overeducation.

Conflict, based on race and class, is a real social phenomenon, and the proposed resolutions depend on which side of the conflict the individual is on. From the perspective of business and political leaders, for example, it makes perfect sense to try to limit four-year college attendance and promote vocational education at community colleges. Why "waste" money on education that most people do not need while at the same time creating unrealistically high aspirations?

Things look different from the perspective of poor and minority students who want to better their lives. It is not enough that some poor and minority individuals can use the community colleges for upward mobility, as Cohen and Brawer (1982) suggest. It is also necessary to look at the opportunity structure for minorities as groups, and for people at different income levels as classes. While vocational education certainly provides limited individual upward mobility, it does little for group mobility.

Community college leaders, therefore, face a dilemma. Do they continue to look at social phenomena from the viewpoints of the leaders of business and government? If so, they will use their institutions to help reproduce race and class inequalities. Do they look at these phenomena from the points of view of their students' desires for upward mobility? If so, they will have to begin considering large-scale social change that goes far beyond the walls of the community college.

References

Breneman, D. W., and Nelson, S. C. *Financing Community Colleges: An Economic Perspective.* Washington, D.C.: Brookings Institution, 1981.

Bureau of Labor Statistics. *Occupational Outlook Handbook, 1982-83 Edition.* Washington, D.C.: U.S. Department of Labor, Bulletin 2200, 1982.

Cohen, A. M., and Brawer, F. B. *The American Community College.* San Francisco: Jossey-Bass, 1982.

Crain, R. L. *The Quality of American High School Graduates: What Personnel Officers Say and Do About It.* Baltimore: Center for Social Organization of Schools, Report #354, The Johns Hopkins University, 1984.

Deegan, W. L., and Drisko, R. "Contract Training: Progress and Policy Issues." *Community and Junior College Journal*, 1985, *55*, 14-17.

Grant, W. V., and Eiden, L. J. *Digest of Education Statistics, 1983-84.* Washington, D.C.: National Center for Education Statistics, 1984.

Greenbaum, J. "Division of Labor in the Computer Field." *Monthly Review*, 1976, *28*, 40-45.

Gross, B., and Gross, R. (Eds.). *The Great School Debate: Which Way for American Education?* New York: Simon and Schuster, 1985.

Grubb, W. N. *The Bandwagon Once More: Vocational Preparation for High Tech Occupations.* Stanford, Calif.: Institute for Research on Educational Finance and Governance, Report #84-B6, Stanford University, 1984.

Grubb, W. N., and Jussaud, D. "Vocationalizing Higher Education: The Causes of Enrollment and Completion in Two-Year Colleges, 1970-1980." Unpublished report, 1985, 47 pp. (ED 258 647)

Maryland State Board for Community Colleges. *Career Development and Job Performance: A Follow-Up Study of Maryland Community College Graduates and Their Employers.* Annapolis, Md.: Maryland State Board for Community Colleges, 1983.

Parnell, D. *The Neglected Majority.* Washington, D.C.: Community College Press, 1985.

Pincus, F. L. "The False Promises of Community Colleges: Class Conflict and Vocational Education." *Harvard Educational Review*, 1980, *50*, 332-361.

Pincus, F. L. "Class Conflict and Community Colleges: Vocational Education During the Reagan Years." *The Review and Proceedings of the Community College Humanities Association*, 1983, *4*, 3-18.

Pincus, F. L. "Customized Contract Training in Community Colleges: Who Really Benefits?" Paper presented at the annual convention of the American Sociological Association, Washington, D.C., August 29, 1985.

Pratzner, F. C. "Look Before You Leap Aboard the Industry/Education Bandwagon." *Voc/Ed*, 1983, *58*, 13-14.

Richardson, R. C., Jr. "Setting an Agenda for Research on the Community Colleges." Paper presented at the annual meeting of the American Educational Research Association, Chicago, April 4, 1985.

Riche, R. W., Hecker, D. E., and Burgan, J. U. "High Technology Today and Tomorrow: A Small Slice of the Employment Pie." *Monthly Labor Review*, 1983, *106*, 50-58.

Rumberger, R. W., and Levin, H. M. *Forecasting the Impact of New Technologies on the Future Job Market*. Stanford, Calif.: Institute for Research on Educational Finance and Governance Report #84-A-4, Stanford University, 1984.

Sheldon, M. S. *Statewide Longitudinal Study: Report on Academic Year 1978-81*. Part 5. *Final Report*. Woodland Hills, Ca.: Los Angeles Pierce College, 1982. 268 pp. (ED 217 917)

Silvestri, G. T., Lukasiewicz, J. M., and Einstein, M. E. "Occupational Employment Projections through 1995." *Monthly Labor Review*, 1983, *106*, 37-49.

Wilms, W. W. *Vocational Education and Social Mobility: A Study of Public and Proprietary School Dropouts and Graduates*. Los Angeles: UCLA Graduate School of Education, 1980.

Wilms, W. W. "Vocational Education and Job Success: The Employer's View." *Phi Delta Kappan*, 1984, *65*, 347-350.

Fred L. Pincus is a sociologist at the University of Maryland.

Continuing education is potentially the most unequal form of higher education.

Lifelong Learning: A New Form of Tracking

L. Steven Zwerling

We can no longer separate the traditional functions of the community college as neatly as in the past—into collegiate, career, compensatory, and community divisions. How does one classify an adult who works full-time and attends intermittently, initially taking skills courses and then credit courses in business, getting an A.A.S. degree in computer technology, and eventually transferring to a four-year college? In effect, this student fits into all four categories.

Traditional definitions are no longer valid. How many students actually take two years to complete work in the two-year college? How many transfer students actually transfer? How many terminal students terminate? Indeed, evidence indicates that more vocational students transfer than academic students do. Why are there now more reverse-transfers than forward transfers?

In a world in which the center no longer holds, where familiar definitions and traditions are obliterated, the brave new world for the community college involves offering a diversity of programs via flexible schedules in a wide variety of formats for adults who move in and out of school as a natural part of their lives. Some seek credentials. Others seek training. Some are in pursuit of recreation. Others pursue love.

They are welcomed on campus by harried administrators looking to fill empty seats and balance tilting budgets. Some faculty are concerned, especially those who feel responsible for upholding the great traditions of the West; after all, what these students seek is considerably less than collegiate. And all of this is viewed quite skeptically by state legislators, who are more and more responsible for funding the activities of two-year colleges. At a time when school lunch programs are being cut, how can they justify providing subsidies for courses like "How to Make Jello-Molds"?

These harried administrators, though, are clever: They convert noncredit courses to credit (and thus continue to receive at least some funding); they enter into contractual relationships with local corporations to provide staff training either on campus or on site; they occasionally garner patron or foundation support for favorite programs. And adult students keep enrolling. In the ten years between 1970 and 1980, part-time student enrollments increased from fewer than 50 percent to more than 60 percent. In the fall of 1984, exactly 65 percent of community college enrollments were part-time ("Fall 1984 Enrollments," 1986).

To embrace this trend, some community college leaders go so far as to advocate converting the colleges into community centers for lifelong learning (Gleazer, 1980). Still others see virtually limitless opportunities for community colleges to provide recurrent education for occupational retraining, academic remediation, and lifelong learning (Deegan, Tillery, and Associates, 1985). Some perceive twelve million professionals in the United States who require continuing education to avoid "knowledge obsolescence" (Hankin and Fey, 1985). There is even one major study that estimates that forty million adults are in the process of making job or career transitions, and that sixty percent of them feel they need additional education to help them make career changes (Arbeiter and others, 1978). Millions more are going through personal transitions—marriage, pregnancy, divorce, relocation, aging, retirement—and community colleges stand ready to offer such courses as "The Secret of Staying in Love," "Having Babies After Thirty," "Living with Children and Maintaining One's Sanity," and "Getting Fired May Be Beneficial to Your Wealth" (Aslanian and Brickell, 1980).

The Social and Economic Consequences of Lifelong Learning

All of this is rather familiar. Less familiar are the social consequences of lifelong learning. It is time to ask this question: What role is continuing education playing to enhance economic and social opportunities for adults? This is a legitimate question, as many claim it is valid to subsidize these programs because they are a significant means of propping the community college's open door wider (Cohen and Brawer, 1982, p. 273).

Does lifelong learning contribute to social mobility, economic justice, and meritocracy? Or does it foster inequality and even economic and social regression? My view is that continuing education may in fact act as a regressive force in our society.

For example, examine the numbers. In 1981, twenty-one million people in the United States were enrolled in courses (13 percent of the total population seventeen years old and older). However, of the twenty-one million, only two million (fewer than 10 percent) were black or Hispanic, and most of these were at lower levels of study in elementary and secondary continuing education programs (Watkins, 1982).

Much of the justification for subsidizing public (and private) education is that schools are the medium through which people achieve positions in society that correspond to their talents and abilities. In recent years, revisionist writers have asserted a different view—that one goal of education is to serve the aspirations of only a few, while reconciling the rest to their places in the social structure. They have attempted to demonstrate that the poor have historically been ill served by the primary and secondary school systems.

Extending that analysis to higher education, I contend there has been little change in people's relative position in the social hierarchy, in spite of the democratization of higher education. The society is just as inequitable as at the turn of the century. To be sure, there have been both income inflation and inflation in credentialing, but there has been little actual reduction in the gap that separates the rich from the middle class or the middle class from the poor. The educational system ritualizes the competition for comparative advantage within the culture. The ritual's final function, however, is to convince people that the resulting inequalities have been fair, partly because schooling has been fair.

The argument for tax-supported education sees schooling as benefiting individuals, as well as society; therefore, all in the society should contribute according to their means to subsidize the participants. Money spent to support education is thought, among other things, to aid an economic redistribution based on merit and achievement. Actually, as many have noted, there is a net flow from poorer citizens to the more affluent as the result of inequities in the tax system and of differences between the affluent and the poor in the amount and quality of education received.

However, compared with continuing education and its distributional effects, other forms of education are quite egalitarian. For example, in traditional forms of postsecondary education, financial aid is available on the basis of need. This is not true for continuing education. Here, financial subsidies are based on achievement: the ability to hold a job and thus be eligible to participate in a tuition-reimbursement plan or to earn enough to pay fees on one's own. And then these costs are often tax-deductible.

The beneficiaries, then, are the "haves," and via their participation in schooling, they consolidate their positions and widen the gap that separates them from the economically marginal.

Other economic beneficiaries are the colleges themselves. First, they receive the income generated by continuing education programs. Then, through these programs, they prepare people to participate in other programs and courses. One thing unites both critics and boosters: The evidence is overwhelming that education leads to more education. In 1981, for example, of the twenty-one million people participating in continuing education, a full forty percent had completed college (Watkins, 1982). There is no better example of how the educational rich get richer.

Adult Development: The Unexamined Consequences

Even the recent excitement about new theories of adult development and how they can help us improve services to adults generally ignore the unexamined consequences. We like it that adult development theory asserts a kind of predictability to a hitherto random art. It also contributes to our own professionalism: We are "andragogues."

There are, however, questions and even problems. If what is said about adult learning and development is valid, then adult classes are more heterogeneous than anything ever before encountered by educators, as these classes are typically populated by students from twenty-five to sixty-five years of age, spanning all levels of adult development. In the face of this, what do we as andragogues do with them, even with our new knowledge of adult learning?

Further, who are the people who have been studied and from whom much of this theory has been deduced? Almost exclusively, they are upper-middle-income white males. The people stepping out of the pop-developmental works (Gail Sheehy's *Passages*, for example) are more Park Avenue than Main Street. More significant, adult developmental psychology in its current state posits a model of adult growth that is almost entirely passive: One passes through the stages of life at predictable times, in predictable order. Active, assertive learning models become obsolete. Life now is an obstacle course. The aim is simply to get through with minimum trouble and pain. Failure means being behind schedule. Any deviation from the norm derives from a pathological source. If something goes wrong, I am not responsible; something must be wrong with my "psychological clock."

Developmentalism becomes an imperative: Change careers! Embark on new marriages via creative divorce! Cut ties to the past! All of this assumes a passive, conservative role for lifelong learning. At most, educators are needed to cheer people on and provide skills for what is inevitable. There is little possibility for social or personal change. The goal of adulthood is merely to survive.

Continuing education may represent the final institutionalization of all learning, from preschool to hospice. Lasch (1978, p. 153) calls this "educationalization," the process whereby all experience becomes a course. Lifelong learning can become a substitute for experience while ironically trying to prepare people for experience. Far from preparing students to live "authentically," the new higher learning can be disabling, leaving people unable to perform the simplest tasks—finding a job, preparing a meal, meeting people, having sex—without instruction.

Lifelong Schooling

Much of the socialization has moved from the family to institutions and experts. Once schools functioned *in loco parentis;* they now serve *in loco familiae.* One institution now offers a Family College, in which parents and children take a course to fly kites together. Another offers "Talk Sex With Teenagers." "Network for Learning" teaches one how to flirt!

Instead of lifelong learning, we may find adults coerced into lifelong schooling. This coercion, from both mandated continuing professional education and from social pressure to raise the level of credentialing, presumably in response to the rising level of skills required for most work, helps perpetuate current class and status distinctions.

Credentials define status; they sort and select people for jobs, determine who will have access to knowledge, and increase dependence not only on experts but also on the educational enterprise itself. Credentials attained via continuing education are generally accessible to those already in the workforce, already schooled, and already confident of their ability to pursue additional schooling. Access also goes to whiter, more affluent individuals. Continuing education, therefore, is potentially the most inequitable segment of organized educational activity: The key entrance requirement (education itself) recapitulates all the inequities in the social structure.

Moreover, the emphasis on career education and responsiveness to local economy, added to the emphasis on the short-term retraining and upgrading of vocational skills (purportedly to enable people to change careers four to six times during a lifetime) does little to foster social mobility.

In these ways, lifelong learning may actually contribute to the maintenance of a floating labor force (in addition to a reserve army of the unemployed), which in the guise of providing opportunities for career change merely enables a person to move about from career to career, without arriving at a destination.

The challenge, then, to continuing educators is articulating a future for our profession that is more equitable and more enfranchising; that encourages voluntary and more intrinsic forms of learning; that emphasizes active learning; and that responds appropriately to the realities people face in the world of work while at the same time encouraging the kind of education that enables people to progress and become more vocationally flexible, so that they can respond to inevitable shifts in the structure of the economy.

Possibilities for Equity

Equity in postsecondary education is generally thought to be served if programs are accessible and affordable, but the programs themselves, much less their outcomes, are rarely considered. Appropriate programming, however, is as important to equity as access and affordability are. *Appropriate programming* here means comprehensive, coherently unified offerings that are carefully designed over the life cycle, offerings that are also designed to take educational background and socioeconomic status into consideration. Programming for equity additionally involves curricular structures that link one educational level to another so as to foster the possibility of continuous progress.

The adult education hierarchy usually separates basic education, job training, continuing professional education, and liberal learning. Progressive notions are not built into this academic plan. Upward movement within this hierarchy occurs only as the result of individual effort, not because of institutional intentions.

A more equitable system would be designed to assist individuals to progress. Rather than offering a hierarchy made up of relatively impervious layers, an equitable system would present a continuous, seamless configuration of offerings in which success at one level would mean direct access to the next.

This conceptualization of lifelong learning yields a literal definition of continuing education—a definition of learning as continuing, a definition of learning that is an education. Too often, continuing education means only courses, workshops, or conferences; little attention is paid to the systematic curricular structures essential to something one might want to call an education. An equitable system, for example, leads to the possibility that many people who earlier missed the chance to enroll, or who were bypassed, could re-enter via a carefully staged program that would speak to their unfolding needs. At the lower levels, this might mean more circumscribed, short-term experiences; at higher levels, it might mean long-term, linked courses and programs that would lead to negotiable credentials.

Affordability changes, too, at different levels. At lower academic and socioeconomic levels, affordability may mean institutional subsidies to students. Equity not only requires that institutions reach out and thereby become accessible to low-income, less well-educated students; equity also requires that institutions invest some of their resources in scholarships and lowered fees. The evidence is clear that this practice, since education leads to more education, might also serve the long-range fiscal interests of institutions.

Lifelong Learning and Social Change

Equity also requires that lifelong learning contribute to social change and to a society where merit, not privilege, is rewarded. Of course, expecting and rewarding excellence is one way to contribute. Another is to realize that the structures of adult curricula and methodologies need not (and, in my view, should not) merely cater to the developmentally predictable needs or capabilities of adults. Educators have a responsibility to motivate and perhaps even prod their students to move beyond normally expected paths of growth. To this end, I am attracted to Mezirow's (1978) notion of "perspective transformation." Through this transformation, adults can come to see how they may be trapped in their own histories. Without a major effort, many may be destined to relive their histories. Carefully considered forms of continuing education can help students become critically aware of the cultural and psychological assumptions that have patterned their lives. In this way, their perspectives can be transformed, and other possibilities for their lives may manifest themselves.

Earlier, I speculated that continuing education may inadvertently act as a regressive force in society and that it is potentially the most inequitable form of organized educational activity. Ironically, just as it has this potential, it also has the potential to play the most progressive role. Having a good education encourages one to continue one's education; continuing education, for the most part (unlike other forms of education), is accessible to all. It generally does not formally screen the students it enrolls; most courses and programs, for example, allow mail and telephone registration. There are few prerequisites other than motivation and confidence.

Of course, it would be naïve to assume casually that people who have not fared well in previous schooling would feel confident about their ability to succeed in programs of continuing education. Acknowledging these psychological and cultural barriers, however, does not negate clear evidence showing that the kinds of people I am concerned about here can and do succeed academically when they participate.

Equity, then, requires that we do a better job of reaching out. This is complicated. It demands, among other things, commitment of resources and development of appropriate programs. It also means dealing with people's consciousness of relationships between the different forms of education and the quality of their lives.

In previous years, many thought that high school graduation would adequately enhance their career chances and enrich their lives in other, less tangible ways. Later, many concluded that a college degree was the necessary credential. More recently, many have pursued graduate and professional degrees for the same reasons. Most recently, there is a belief among many people that lifelong learning is the key to success and a rich life.

In some communities, however, it is still felt that the college degree is the crucial credential. Although obviously important in itself, it rarely leads now to the kinds of rewards envisioned. Indeed, many adults who later in life earn undergraduate degrees are disappointed when they gain no automatic access to new or enhanced careers. They encounter age discrimination, certainly, but they also find that employers, looking for more than the "piece of paper," seek the kinds of competencies best gained via continuing education.

Thus, people in communities that have traditionally been bypassed, in spite of the expansion of educational opportunities, have the chance to use the new opportunities presented by lifelong learning. If they understand the shifting history of the relationships between levels of education and career and life enhancement, then they can directly and immediately enter the sector of education that currently offers the richest rewards.

The most substantial barriers to access are those of our own devising. This is both the bad news and the good. Ultimately, the picture must be viewed optimistically, as the obstacles that need to be removed are in the hands of all of us.

References

Arbeiter, S., Aslanian, C. B., Schmerback, F. A., and Brickell, H. M. *Forty Million Americans in Career Transition: The Need for Information.* New York: College Entrance Examination Board, 1978.

Aslanian, C. B., and Brickell, H. M. *Americans in Transition: Life Changes as Reasons for Adult Learning.* New York: College Entrance Examination Board, 1980.

Cohen, A. M., and Brawer, F. B. *The American Community College.* San Francisco: Jossey-Bass, 1982.

Deegan, W. L., Tillery, D., and Associates. *Renewing the American Community College: Priorities and Strategies for Effective Leadership.* San Francisco: Jossey-Bass, 1985.

"Fall 1984 Enrollments." *Chronicle of Higher Education,* January 22, 1986, p. 26.

Gleazer, E. J., Jr. *The Community College: Values, Vision, and Vitality.* Washington, D.C.: American Association of Community and Junior Colleges, 1980.

Hankin, J. N., and Fey, P. A. "Reassessing the Commitment to Community Services." In W. L. Deegan, D. Tillery, and Associates, *Renewing the American Community College: Priorities and Strategies for Effective Leadership.* San Francisco, Jossey-Bass, 1985.

Lasch, C. *The Culture of Narcissism.* New York: Norton, 1978.

Mezirow, J. "Perspective Transformation." *Adult Education,* 1978, *28* (2), 100–110.

Watkins, B. T. "21 Million Adults Found Taking Part in Continuing Education Programs." *Chronicle of Higher Education,* May 5, 1982, p. 8.

L. Steven Zwerling is associate dean of New York University's School of Continuing Education and author of Second Best: The Crisis of the Community College.

*The open-door community college offers less access to
upward mobility and economic status for minorities than its
proponents claim or its history justifies.*

Minority Students and the Community College

Reginald Wilson

The conventional wisdom that higher education leads to a better life, especially for minority students, is a generally accepted article of faith among most Americans. Indeed, a casual reading of history seems to justify that faith and to support reliance on education as the path to upward mobility and economic status in society.

At the turn of the century, high schools were seen as providing literacy and vocational training to the masses of immigrants arriving from Europe. Subsequently, such colleges as the City College of New York were designated the "Harvards of the proletariat" in making access to higher learning and the professions a reality for the children of these immigrants (Lavin and others, 1979). Colleges were presumed to lead the masses out of poverty and to create social mobility among the classes, thus fulfilling the American dream of equal opportunity for all. Indeed, the brilliant achievements of many graduates of City College seemed to reinforce those possibilities for all Americans.

Nevertheless, what colleges appeared to do for European immigrants they did not do for the similar aspirations of blacks, Puerto Ricans, Mexican-Americans, and other nonwhite migrants to the urban centers in the second half of the century. Stringent college-entrance requirements and lower economic resources served to limit access to higher education for predominantly lower-class minorities and to create barriers to whatever upward mobility was available as a consequence of postsecondary training. An ideological tension regarding the issue of access and achievement exists among commentators on education's contribution to social class mobility. Some of these commentators believe education does indeed allow substantial upward mobility for those who gain access to its benefits; others insist that the educational system merely reinforces the class and economic positions of the various status groups in society. Both camps agree that the overwhelming majority of nonwhites, for whatever reasons, have been conspicuously absent from the benefits of higher education.

After World War II

The period immediately following World War II was one of burgeoning opportunities for postsecondary educational attainment. The World War II G.I. Bill (and subsequent Korean and Vietnam Bills) enabled tens of thousands of veterans to have access to higher education, including many whose previous educational and economic status would have precluded such access. A decade of social and civil rights legislation followed in the 1960s and extended educational opportunities to thousands of ordinary citizens with educational and economic limitations similar to those of many veterans. One need only recite some of the names and dates: The 1964 Civil Rights Act; the 1965 Affirmative Action Executive Order 11246; the 1967 Executive Order 11375 prohibiting sex discrimination; the 1971 Basic Educational Opportunity (Pell) Grants; and the 1972 *Adams* decision dismantling segregated higher education. Concurrent with this period was the exponential growth of community colleges. For example, in 1960 there were only 678 community colleges, with an enrollment of 660,216. By 1971 there were 1,111 community colleges, with 2,680,762 students—a near-doubling of the number of institutions and quadrupling of students (de los Santos, 1980, p. 6).

Increase in Numbers

In the heady atmosphere of the 1960s and that decade's progressive social climate, the community colleges were perceived as perhaps providing for ethnic minorities and the poor the same benefits and mobility as were available for the preceding generation of European immigrants. Indeed, in the optimistic 1960s, the community colleges, with their expanding career and technical programs, were touted as being on the cutting edge of postsecondary training and more relevant to work-force needs than the traditional four-year liberal arts colleges were.

Certainly, the period coinciding with the civil rights movement saw a veritable explosion of access to higher education for minorities, with the removal of many economic barriers and of pernicious barriers of racial segregation in Southern colleges. In 1960, there were approximately 600,000 blacks in college, and 65 percent of those were in historically black colleges. By 1980, there were nearly 1.2 million blacks in college, of whom over 80 percent were in predominantly white institutions (Wilson and Melendez, 1985, p. 18). In 1976, there were 383,000 Hispanics in college, and the number increased to 519,000 by 1982 (Wilson and Melendez, 1985, p. 7). The social climate of the 1960s was part of a worldwide phenomenon of rising expectations, in which Third World and disadvantaged people made demands on nations and institutions, expecting equal representation. Indeed, the initial dramatic gains in minority numbers seemed to ensure that the goal of parity would come close to realization within the lifetime of that 1960s generation.

The institutions of higher education proved remarkably resilient in absorbing these demands for change while remaining considerably unchanged in their fundamental organization. An analysis of the distribution of minorities within these institutions finds them heavily concentrated on the periphery of higher education.

Despite the dramatic increase in overall numbers, 41 percent of black students are in community colleges, as are 53 percent of Hispanics, compared to 33 percent of whites (Wilson and Melendez, 1983, p. 10). While numbering over 12 percent in the general population, blacks represent only 4.2 percent of higher education faculties, and half of those faculty members are in the historically black colleges. Hispanics, who constitute over 6 percent of the population, comprise only 1.6 percent of the faculties. These numbers represent a decline for blacks since 1979 and a plateau for Hispanics (Wilson and Melendez, 1985, p. 17). Blacks declined in representation in administrative positions during the same period; again, Hispanics plateaued. The tenuousness of minority representation in all segments of the academy—student bodies, faculties, administrations—remained relatively unchanged during the period of most vigorous activity. A survey of college presidents' views of the importance of recruiting minority students revealed that concern to be at 47 percent for doctoral institutions, 40 percent at comprehensive colleges, and 35 percent at community colleges. These numbers are in inverse relationship to the actual presence of minorities in these respective student bodies. Despite the expressions of concern, the proportional representation of minorities has remained unchanged; indeed, in the past decade representation has declined (College Presidents' Views. . . , 1985).

Withdrawal rates for minority students from community colleges are significantly higher than for white students (and most withdrawals are for nonacademic reasons). Consequently, completion of associate degrees is low for minorities, despite their overrepresentation in community colleges. For example, while whites make up 75 percent of community college students, they attain 85 percent of the associate degrees. Blacks, at 13 percent, attain only 8 percent of the degrees; Hispanics, at 6 percent, attain 4 percent of the degrees (de los Santos, 1980, p. 25). Since minorities' curriculum choices are concentrated in career and vocational programs, there are significantly fewer in academic programs who will transfer to four-year institutions. Thus, despite the increase in numbers of minorities in colleges, the minority attainment of associate degrees is modest, and the subsequent attainment of baccalaureate degrees remains relatively unchanged (Wilson and Melendez, 1984, p. 8).

It is important to state at this juncture that we recognize the comprehensive mission of the community college. The point of this analysis is to determine whether the dramatic increase in minority participation in higher education during the 1960s and 1970s contributed to a significant change in economic and social class mobility for minorities. Our findings suggest that it did not. While opportunity and access increased considerably, success, measured as outcomes in degree attainment that subsequently affected class and economic position, was rather modest and continued to characterize minorities on the whole as substantially underrepresented in the economy.

Reasons for Limited Impact

Explanations for the limited progress of minorities in higher education generally, and in community colleges particularly, are several and of unequal value. Nevertheless, four principal ones seem to be significant in contributing to our understanding the complexities of the situation.

Economic and Social Policy Shifts. Up to the 1970s, the community college curriculum was predominantly academic in its course offerings (over 70 percent). This was significantly reversed during the 1970s following the passage of the Vocational Education Amendments of 1968 and the subsequent availability of millions of federal dollars for occupational education in community colleges. With these funds, supplemented by state and local matching grants, the community colleges took over from high schools the primary role in offering career and technical education (Baron, 1984, pp. 35-36). This major movement occurred simultaneously with the rise in unemployment among baccalaureate graduates and with the increasing attractiveness of career training programs. This shift in emphasis in program offerings also coincided with the upsurge in enrollments that was occurring in community colleges. Since minority students were already overrepresented in general and vocational tracks in high schools, their subsequent enrollment in community colleges was understandably high in similar programs (Wilson and Melendez, 1983, p. 7). However, students who major in vocational curricula are significantly less likely to graduate or transfer to four-year schools than are their counterparts in liberal arts programs (Lavin and others, 1979, p. 77). Overrepresentation of minorities in vocational programs increases the likelihood that they will not complete their degrees or transfer.

Entering Student Characteristics. "Black and Hispanic students are more likely to be placed in nonacademic high school tracks, and this has important consequences for their subsequent education. One study found that track in high school was more important than ability in determining whether students went to college or, if they did, whether they enrolled in a four-year or two-year institution" (Lavin and others, 1979, p. 71). Only 33 percent of black students and 27 percent of Hispanic students take academic programs in high school, yet nearly 80 percent of minority students express some interest in postsecondary education while at the same time lacking the academic preparation to qualify for admission to the most selective colleges.

Compounding minorities' limited preparation for college work is the inferior quality of their preparation in and of itself. Most commentators on the effectiveness of inner-city high schools note the substantially lower achievement of students in those schools, which is related both to the poor quality of those schools and to the inadequate primary school preparation of students entering those schools. Studies of inner-city high schools reveal fewer teachers per 1,000 students, poorer preparation of those teachers at the colleges they attended, and fewer counseling and equipment resources. Many of these high schools do not even offer a basic precollegiate curriculum (Orfield and others, 1984, p. viii). The most inferior schools serve student bodies that are predominantly minority and poor. Comparable suburban high schools have achievement scores well above the national norm, and a majority of their students are in academic programs.

Counselors to minority students in nonacademic programs very likely perceive these students "to be poor material for higher education and counsel them accordingly" (Lavin and others, 1979, p. 72). The consequences of this kind of counseling undoubtedly affect student choices of postsecondary programs; thus, minority students tend to self-select less rigorous college programs and apply to less elite institutions. Over one-third of black and Hispanic high school graduates who apply for postsecondary education indicate that they will need remedial assistance in basic skills. Obviously, it becomes increasingly difficult at each stage of the educational process to overcome "the cumulative impact of past inequalities" (Lavin and others, 1979, p. 86). Therefore, and this is not surprising, the primary beneficiaries of even open-admission institutions are the better-prepared white students, rather than minorities.

Institutional Barriers. The "age of excellence" arrived just as minority students were making measurable progress in academic achievement, after twenty years of national decline in Scholastic Aptitude Test (SAT) scores. That decline stopped in 1982, primarily because of the marked improvement in the SAT scores of blacks and Hispanics, and improvement continued for the next three years. Nevertheless, despite the improvement, the average SAT scores of minorities are still significantly lower than those of white students, averaging 215 points lower for blacks and 136 points lower for Hispanics.

As of mid-1985, nearly twenty states have raised high school graduation requirements, either through more stringent curriculum requirements or by requiring exit tests, and nearly thirty states have increased admissions standards for state colleges and universities (Mitgang, 1985, p. 1). Since minority performance on standardized tests is typically lower than that of white students, the raising of required test scores is a direct prescription of educational failure for a considerable number of minority students. As more than one investigator has suggested, "raising standards tends to benefit those students who already perform well but doesn't seem to make a difference for students who perform poorly" (Lewis, 1985, p. 252). One would only add the caveat that raising standards does not make a difference *only* if no change in teaching strategies or enrichment of learning experiences is provided for minority students.

The increased use of testing is occurring even in the open-door community colleges, prompting the observation that the front door may be open but many of the rooms may be locked (Wilson and Melendez, 1985, pp. 20-21). A survey by the American College Testing Program documented the increasing use of tests in community colleges to screen admission to many technical and occupational programs. As a result, it is not surprising to find, even in many community colleges with predominantly minority student bodies, that the students in such "elite" programs as nursing, electronics, and pre-engineering are mostly white (Wilson, 1985, p. 3). Thus, the open-door community college can be as stratified as the rest of society.

There is a consequential body of evidence substantiating that when appropriate remedial and compensatory assistance is provided, minority students are capable of performing at or above standards of competency (Wilson, 1985, p. 8). However, the trend in recent years, both at federal and state levels, is for funds to be reduced for remedial and compensatory programs (Lewis, 1985, p. 251-252). Again, it is clear that raising standards without providing resources to meet them is a direct prescription for failure.

Changes in National Climate and Federal Policy. The national mood of support for progressive social legislation to end official segregation and reverse the historic and pervasive discriminatory practices against minorities began to decline as early as the late 1960s. A 1971 survey of Americans found, in response to conditions leading to race riots, that 52 percent of white males favored "stronger police control" rather than the improvement of "Negro conditions" (Campbell, 1971, p. 29). The same survey found the attitudes of white college students to be most in support of social justice. Indeed, in 1970, 69.2 percent of entering community college freshmen said that "developing a philosophy of life" was their most important goal; by 1980, only 44.6 percent of them gave this goal priority, while the overwhelming majority chose "being well-off financially" as their paramount goal (Baron, 1984, p. 36). Policy makers in Washington became increasingly disillusioned with what seemed to be the intractable nature of the social problems of the disadvantaged, which appeared relatively unchanged by the billions of dollars poured into Great Society programs. Some policy makers suggested a hiatus, a "benign neglect." Others suggested that compensatory educational programs addressing the deficiencies of the disadvantaged were doomed to failure because those deficiencies were genetic rather than susceptible to positive environmental enrichment.

Although the societal commitment to equity diminished under successive administrations, no presidential administration attempted to systematically dismantle the various social programs until President Reagan took office in 1981. No administration was ever so ideologically committed to eliminating all such programs or moved so swiftly to do so. Every budget submitted by the Reagan administration recommended either elimination of or substantial reductions in funds for such programs as the Pell Grants, Upward Bound, TRIO Programs, affirmative action, bilingual education, Title I, compensatory education, and even school lunches. Despite the resistance of Congress to the most draconian cuts that were recommended, the decline of the past four years (including the impact of the budget deficit) is measurable and substantial.

Between 1980 and 1984, the share of national income received by the lowest fifth of the population (where most minorities are) declined from 4.9 percent to 4.7 percent. Between 1980 and 1984, the availability of grants as a percentage of total financial aid declined from 55 percent to 41 percent. Between 1980 and 1984, available financial aid declined by 21 percent in constant dollars. Between 1980 and 1984, college tuition increased by over 12 percent (Wilson and Melendez, 1985, p. 21). The Reagan administration has opposed student grants, preferring self-help (defined as work-study and loans) as the major way of financing college education. With their diminished economic viability, minorities have been reluctant to shift from grants to loans. As a consequence, an increasing proportion of student aid dollars goes to middle-class white students, rather than to minorities and to the poor, whom the assistance programs were originally intended to help.

From 1975 to 1982, a direct consequence of these policies, compounding the other barriers described above, has been declining participation in higher education among blacks, by 11 percent, and among Hispanics, by 16 percent (Wilson and Melendez, 1984, p. 10). Community college enrollment among minorities has also declined overall, and in some states the decline is astonishing. In California, for example, black enrollment in community colleges declined by 17 percent in 1984 alone ("California Community College Chief . . . ," 1985). Continued declines of this nature, or even the maintenance of the current considerable underrepresentation, can have serious long-term social and economic consequences.

Conclusion

There are lessons to be learned from this survey of the involvement of minorities in community colleges. First, it must be noted that this chapter has dealt exclusively with blacks and Hispanics, who make up well over 90 percent of American minorities. (The experiences of Native Americans and Asians are different enough to take us far afield from the central thrust of this chapter. Nevertheless, "new" Asian immigrants suffer from many of the same problems as blacks and Hispanics.)

The experiences of American racial minorities cannot be meaningfully compared with those of European immigrants, whose socialization and absorption into the majority white population did not involve the historical barriers of slavery, legal discrimination, and the pervasive racial prejudice that continues to plague nonwhite minorities in their encounters with every institution of American life. Moreover, European immigrants established a significant economic base before their second and succeeding generations enjoyed widespread higher educational advantage. Blacks and Hispanics have no substantial economic base, and each generation produces its "first" generation of college students (except for the small middle class of these groups).

The euphoria of the 1960s, and the early expectation of rapid minority assimilation through the open-door community colleges, were simplistic and mistaken. Indeed, the community colleges did provide open access, but the avenues to upward mobility, technical education, and transfer to baccalaureate institutions were substantially blocked by the inadequacies of minority secondary school preparation, as well as by the high standards and criteria of admission and exit, to which minorities themselves often acquiesced, without the accompanying remedial and compensatory measures necessary to meet those standards and criteria. (Acceptance of majority definitions of one's colonized status is the first requirement of maintaining colonialism.)

The position of minorities in community colleges can be understood only in the wider context of the pervasive societal limitations on upward mobility. Institutions and social structures do tend to reproduce the class and economic positions of citizens and serve to maintain the status quo, despite appearances of change. These institutions most readily accommodate pressures to change by changing only peripherally and leaving the principal control, authority, and rules intact. The "demands" of minorities in the 1960s were responded to by the creation of peripheral structures—special projects, TRIO, Upward Bound, and urban community colleges. These left the centrality of power, and the rules by which power is exercised and allocated, relatively undisturbed. To change societal institutions, we must reorganize them with different rules and criteria of power allocation.

Blacks and Hispanics are the fastest-growing groups in American society. The combination of high birthrates and immigration will produce a cohort constituting 35 percent of the American population shortly after the year 2000. Until recently, minorities languishing at the bottom of society could be viewed with anguish, but not as a phenomenon impinging on the central concerns of American society. However, if one-third of the population continues to decline in higher education participation and economic capability, that condition can only lead to social and economic apartheid. Morality aside, it is in the long-term self-interest of American society not to let that occur. This is an old message. However, no data exist to persuade us that the message is less true than when it was first articulated over 120 years ago, in the Thirteenth, Fourteenth, and Fifteenth amendments to the United States Constitution.

References

Baron, R. F. "Why the Big Change in Student Program Selection at Two-Year Colleges?" *Educational Record*, 1984, Winter, 35-36.

"California Community College Chief Wants to Turn System Around." *Black Issues in Higher Education*, December 1, 1985, p. 4.

Campbell, A. *White Attitudes Toward Black People.* Ann Arbor: Institute for Social Research, the University of Michigan, 1971.

"College Presidents' Views on Trends and Issues." *Chronicle of Higher Education*, December 4, 1985, p. 42.

de los Santos, A. G., Jr. *Hispanics and Community Colleges.* Topical Paper no. 18. Tucson: University of Arizona, January 1980.

Lavin, D. E., Alba, R. D., and Silberstein, R. A. "Open Admissions and Equal Access: A Study of Ethnic Groups in the City University of New York." *Harvard Educational Review*, 1979, *1* (49), 53-92.

Lewis, A. "Young and Poor in America." *Phi Delta Kappan*, 1985, 67 (4), 251-252.

Mitgang, I. "Educators Still Grading Results of Recent Avalanche of Testing." *Washington Times*, August 24, 1985, p. 1.

Orfield, G., and others. *The Chicago Study of Access and Choice in Higher Education.* Chicago: University of Chicago, September 1984. 351 pp. (ED 248 929)

Wilson, R. "Minority Students in Community Colleges: Future Crises." Paper presented at the Association of Community College Trustees Conference, Denver, October 4, 1985.

Wilson, R., and Melendez, S. E. *Second Annual Status Report: Minorities in Higher Education.* Washington, D.C.: American Council on Education, 1983.

Wilson, R., and Melendez, S. E. *Third Annual Status Report: Minorities in Higher Education.* Washington, D.C.: American Council on Education, 1984.

Wilson, R., and Melendez, S. E. *Fourth Annual Status Report: Minorities in Higher Education.* Washington, D.C.: American Council on Education, 1985.

Reginald Wilson is director of the Office of Minority Concerns of the American Council on Education. He is the former president of Wayne County Community College and is the editor of Race and Equity in Higher Education.

Although women represent nearly 60 percent of community college enrollments, curricular stereotyping and the lack of appropriate student services lead to unequal results.

A Place for Women?

Marilyn Gittell

Conflicting ideologies and goals in American education are reflected in the institutional development of higher education and the expectations of critics and consumers. Theorists disagree as to the role of education. Functionalists see the education system as a product of the system, a preserver of the status quo (Bowles and Gintis, 1976). Others see education in America as a progressive force, the equalizer of populations, providing opportunities for mobility within the society (Cremin, 1961; Ravitch, 1983). Confusion in the literature abounds because the analysts sometimes fail to distinguish their analysis of what the education system "is" from what they think it "should be." Often disagreement suggests the difference between expectations and reality—what education could achieve for the society, as contrasted with what it is doing. Some of the major reformers are the same people who see education as a product of the economic system, narrowing the possibilities for change. Those who claim education has served an important political function, addressing the needs of new populations in the society, often defend the status quo function of education. In the history of higher education, these conflicting elements are evident. Rudolf (1962), a major historian of higher education, concludes that the higher education system is in fact not a system, because it has responded to increased demands in each era not by adjusting existing institutions but by creating new institutions to serve new populations.

Each of these new classes of institutions (land grant colleges, black

L. S. Zwerling (Ed.). *The Community College and Its Critics.*
New Directions for Community Colleges, no. 54. San Francisco: Jossey-Bass, June 1986.

colleges, women's colleges, urban Catholic colleges) adjusts the curriculum to suit its own special populations. Therefore, there is not even an accepted definition of what constitutes a liberal arts education (Hacker, 1986). There are those who persist, however, in assuming that there is or should be a single approach for all higher education institutions, ignoring not only this history but also the character of student populations and their differences in background and needs.

Community colleges can be viewed as the most recent group of institutions established to serve an unserved population whose needs were not met by the existing institutions. The growth of these colleges, from 593 in 1960 to 1,281 in 1982, reflects increased pressure to provide access to higher education to large numbers of students who were denied access to the existing system. The growth took place largely in the public sector. Enrollments in these two-year public institutions grew from 393,553 in 1960 to 4,494,202 in 1982. Who were these students? In all two-year institutions, the percentage of women grew, from 38 percent of the student population to 56 percent. The number of part-time students increased, from 284,271 in 1963 to 2,848,333 in 1982 (American Council on Education, 1984).

The Urban Community College

Urban community colleges, more than any other group of higher education institutions, have an unusually large population of women who are part-time students. Although precise national data are not available, a high proportion of these new women students are likely to be older, single parents, minority, and from lower-income groups. Data for the City University of New York community colleges, for example, indicate that in 1982 women comprised 70 percent of the student population, and black and Hispanic students were 63.5 percent of the student population (this contrasts to 1969, when 30 percent of the community college population was black and Hispanic) (Alvarado, 1985). In a recent Ford Foundation program to encourage urban community college transfer programs, numerous colleges qualified for the program because the majority of their student populations were minority students. It is important to distinguish these urban community colleges as a class of institutions because their populations are so distinctive and their contrast with suburban middle-class colleges is so great. Unfortunately, none of the data collectors have distinguished these colleges from the category of two-year colleges, with which they have little in common. This general identification of the urban two-year colleges with the other two-year institutions may in fact contribute to the failure of the urban community colleges to recognize that they are different and must concern themselves with the very special needs of their students.

Urban community colleges in the larger cities must face the reality that 50 percent to 70 percent of high school students are minority, more than

50 percent drop out before they graduate, and many will ultimately seek to re-enter school via the community colleges. In a recent study I conducted for the Ford Foundation, I interviewed ninety-five lower-income minority women in education programs in three cities and found that their preparation for college was poor if not totally inadequate. Many were school dropouts but entered special programs and attained GEDs. (At the City University community colleges in 1982, 14 percent of first-time freshmen were GED students.) A large number can recall traumatic experiences in high school that led them to leave school. An unusually large number expressed particular difficulty with taking tests. Their aspirations for postsecondary education were high. They faced basic needs. Most pressing were financial support, childcare, and medical services for their families (Gittell, 1985b). These needs must be addressed if these women are to be served by higher education. The general data available for community college students confirm my own findings that women students are more dependent on financial aid than male students are (Astin and others, 1985).

The urban community colleges have more in common with four-year urban institutions than with their two-year counterparts in suburban and rural areas. The four-year colleges have the advantage of being able to distinguish the smaller numbers of older, minority women students from the younger, more traditional college population. They can and often do address the particular needs of groups of nontraditional students with special programs, services, sympathetic faculty, course scheduling, and counseling. They prefer to distinguish this discretely different population, often quite limited in size, from the rest of their students. The University of Massachusetts at Boston runs a well-regarded program for AFDC women in which the group of students is accorded special treatment, functions as a supportive group, and gets special counseling and flexible scheduling. Roxbury Community College, in contrast, serves a population almost totally made up of older minority women; the entire character of the college would have to change if it were to recognize the distinctive character of the population it was created to serve. Roxbury is a college created by grass-roots community activists in the 1960s to serve the local population in more responsive ways. Its conversion from a private, community-based neighborhood college to a public institution seemed to foster a more conservative and traditional view of its programs and services. The pressure to fit into a model of a postsecondary institution and assume that there are distinctive and universal characteristics that define higher education institutions is great, even in the face of contradictory historical evidence.

The Struggle For Status

Struggling to attain status in the larger world of higher education, urban community colleges are inclined to behave as if they were in fact more like all other institutions. One community college president in a large East Coast city informed me that her board and faculty did not want to move in the direction of serving a nontraditional population of older, low-income minority women. They did not see that as their mission. Several community-based colleges and programs have been established in that city to serve those women, many of whom dropped out of public community colleges, which treated them like traditional students. In a study of urban community-based colleges (1985a), I discovered that the proliferation of those colleges was a response to city populations who were poorly served by the large public community colleges. The students we interviewed for that study, many of whom dropped out of the community colleges, attributed their lack of success to the size of those colleges, bureaucratic red tape, the lack of interest in or attention to their need for extra counseling for financial aid and program development, their own ineffective basic skills and remedial work, and the unsympathetic attitudes of most of the faculty. In the community-based colleges, they found smaller class size, more flexible class scheduling, more likelihood of daycare facilities, close attention to financial aid, and a more sympathetic faculty. Our field visits and interviews, conducted at the community-based colleges, confirmed that these colleges were thoughtfully developing programs that responded to many of those needs. The coeducational community-based colleges with overwhelmingly large number of minority women students did not develop peer-group support systems and nontraditional programs to address the fundamental problem of sex stereotyping, which restricts the opportunities of women students. This is also the major failure of urban community colleges.

The reality is that although community colleges are forced to accept their roles as open-access institutions, they do little to retain students, broaden their educational experiences, encourage and prepare them for transfer to four-year programs, or prepare them for more upwardly mobile careers (Karabel, 1972). It has become acceptable practice to live with a dropout rate of over 70 percent in these colleges. Astin and Snyder (1982) reported that nine years after entering a two-year college, only one out of four students had attained a B.A. degree. Unfortunately, the data do not distinguish results by gender, and so we cannot determine whether women suffer any more than men from this limited success with preparing students for transfer to four-year programs. Admittedly, community college registrations do include large numbers of students who may be seeking single courses or limited educational experiences, so that the numbers are somewhat skewed; however, three out of four freshmen in two-year colleges state that they plan to go on to a four-year degree. Many of those students probably have little comprehension of what is entailed in completing a degree, but one would have to conclude from the results that the community colleges do little to give them a better perspective. A survey of urban community college students and faculty by Bensimon (1986) found a wide disparity in students' views of transfer programs. The faculty in large numbers did not think they should encourage their students to consider transfer programs, while a high percentage of the students saw themselves as transfer students.

Gender Stereotyping

In the area of curriculum, community colleges do their greatest damage to women. Community college emphasis on job-oriented vocational programs, highly touted as the realistic approach to their students' needs and skills, has very negative results, especially for women. The heavy concentration on these vocational programs and the channeling of major resources into them short-changes the liberal arts programs, which can offer broader educational experiences and opportunities for transfer to four-year colleges. Course scheduling is less flexible and course requirements are more restrictive.

A variety of studies suggest that high school students follow gender stereotyping in their selection of courses and careers and that counseling in secondary schools contributes to those early decisions. The community colleges not only do not make any effort to break through those stereotypes, they often reinforce them in their own counseling and curricula. In an effort to demonstrate the narrow tracking of women students into traditional study and career patterns, we requested data from several urban community colleges on gender distribution among majors. Most of the colleges do not even collect data by gender, which in itself suggests a lack of sensitivity to the issue. When the data are available, they demonstrate the highly skewed concentration of women at the bottom end—in business programs, in secretarial studies, in nursing, and in the lower-end health and human services subprofessional career programs. Men dominate the more technical fields and the upper-end business and subengineering programs. The latter jobs tend to be the ones that offer greater social mobility.

Many of the vocational programs have selective admissions; nursing programs, in particular, have developed screening devices that often exclude large numbers of women. The poor preparation of women in math and science in high school makes them ineligible for some of the technical two-year programs. College counselors direct women into the areas where women have traditionally worked. In a limited survey of urban public two-year colleges, we found only one experimental program specifically designed to prepare women in nontraditional areas. The program was funded by a foundation and has not yet been expanded to the general college program. National data on associate degrees awarded suggest the pervasive character of these practices in community colleges. If community colleges do not make a special effort to reverse these policies, they contribute to the reinforcement of gender stereotyping, which severely limits both educational advancement and employment opportunities for women. Some community college officials justify these policies by noting that they are realistic and respond to job market opportunities. Others, including some feminist critics (Bers, 1983), use the rationale that the projected increase in jobs is greatest in the areas of highest current female employment, and community college programs should be job-directed. There seems to be little concern that these jobs are the lowest-paying jobs and provide the least mobility for women. In some cases, for example in secretarial services, many of the current jobs will be eliminated by automation.

Fuchs (1983) attributes the significant wage differential between men and women to gender-specific role differentiation and suggests that unless women are educated and trained to enter the fields previously reserved for men, they will continue to have more limited work opportunities and will be forced into lower-paying jobs. Fuchs also concludes that "greater equality in occupational structure is probably the most important step toward greater equality in earnings between men and women" (Fuchs, 1983).

There are several successful education programs that train women in nontraditional fields. A private institution, the Womens Technical College in Boston, has been offering a program for women in drafting and electronic computer technology. The college was originally funded by the Ford Foundation and is now self-supporting. The Womens Technical College program has an arrangement with Roxbury Community College to use its computers. All the women who have completed the program—and the retention rate far exceeds percentages for the community colleges—have been placed in jobs with salaries averaging $12,000. The women in the program are typical of the urban community college population. In interviews with program participants conducted in 1985, they told us that the program environment provided strong peer-group support. In addition, they viewed the attitude of the staff, the smaller class size, and the special remedial work as the most positive aspects of the program and reasons for its success. Many of these women were dropouts from larger public institutions. This fact strongly suggests that urban community colleges might consider peer-group support and smaller class size as vital to addressing the needs of this constituency. The most effective way to achieve these goals would be to create public urban women's community colleges specifically designed to adopt new approaches to the particular problems faced by this growing population of women students.

Women in Higher Education

Howe (1984) has outlined three major periods in the struggle for change in women's higher education. The earliest efforts were directed at training women as teachers. Women were to be educated separately from men, given differences between the sexes and specific concerns of teaching as a profession. The curriculum reflected the limited intention of training women for domestic life and for a brief teaching career. As Howe suggests, "They learned enough to teach rudiments to others, not to shape knowledge anew." Needless to say, the women who were recruited to assume these roles were from upper- and middle-income backgrounds, and the colleges they attended were elite women's colleges. In the second phase, the emphasis was on securing the same education for women as men had established for themselves. There was a vocational goal—training women for careers in medicine, engineering, and so on. In practice, the few small liberal arts colleges and larger land grant colleges that admitted women allowed them to take liberal arts courses but restricted their career training to women's careers, primarily in home economics, social work, nursing, and teaching. These were mostly middle-class women, although some were from working-class backgrounds. Howe views the third and most recent phase of higher education for women as largely influenced by the development of women's studies, which concerns itself with curriculum content in all areas and with challenges to male-dominated fields. She sees a major effort by the feminist movement as necessary to urge women to enter these fields and to reform institutions so that they will be more receptive to training women to enter these nontraditional fields.

It is clear that the urban community colleges need the pressure of outside forces to make the changes Howe is seeking. In the past, we could look to government support as a catalyst for change in educational institutions. That is certainly less likely now. Although the Perkins Vocational Educational Bill, passed by Congress in 1985, did make extensive provisions for funding nontraditional training and education programs for women, it left to the states the development of master plans to implement the legislation. In workshops conducted throughout the country, participants expressed pessimism that community colleges would be a significant source of change; they looked instead to community-based institutions and to new programs sensitive to the needs of lower-income, minority women.

In the 1960s and the 1970s, the civil rights and women's movements were instrumental in pressuring for the expansion of affirmative action policies and programs in higher education institutions. They succeeded in raising the consciousness of many people regarding the discriminatory practices prevalent in colleges and universities. Studies and reports were commissioned to explore the problems of women in higher education. Recommendations were generally consistent, suggesting increased funding of special programs and services for the increasing number of women students. Primary among recommendations was to increase the number of women administrators and faculty. Daycare, women's studies, women's centers, flexible scheduling, continuing education, career counseling, and nontraditional career programs were all seen as important to women students. Many of these changes were even more essential to the new older, lower-income, and minority women students. Bers (1983) and Dziech (1983) evaluate community college achievements in most of these areas as minimal.

Touchton and Shavlik (1984) note that the number of senior women adminstrators has increased in all institutions between 1975 and 1983: "Although liberal arts colleges still employ more senior administrators than any other type of institution, women in two-year institutions moved from representing 24 percent of the total to 31 percent of the total." The number of women presidents in public two-year colleges, including a number of minority women, increased from eleven in 1975 to seventy-two in 1984. These data may reflect growth in the size and number of two-year colleges rather than more enlightened policies. According to Astin and Snyder (1982), although women hold more faculty positions in community colleges than they do in four-year institutions, they are generally clustered in the lower ranks, and their salaries still are only 81.9 percent of comparable salaries for males. In addition, women faculty members, like their students, are overrepresented in the humanities, education, nursing, and human services.

Urban Women's Colleges

The data suggest that community colleges have not been outstanding in the creation of daycare facilities or women's centers and have not been so receptive to women's studies as the four-year liberal arts colleges have been. In continuing education, one might expect community colleges to have created innovative programs because so many of their students take noncredit and single courses, but the urban community colleges have been more traditional in their offerings than four-year colleges have been, and public institutions in many cities are less forward-thinking than private institutions are. Special career counseling, responsive financial aid programs, and women's support programs are also rare. Bers (1983) also notes the relative lack of women on community college boards of trustees as a limiting factor in making community colleges more responsive to the needs of women students.

It seems that the community colleges have not become places where the new women students can find particular sensitivity to their needs. Efforts to reform those institutions may be a losing battle. In the tradition of American higher education, it is probably more productive to create new institutions—urban women's colleges—to take on the task.

References

Alvarado, A. *Toward Reshaping the Mission and Vision of New York City's Community Colleges.* New York: Center for Public Advocacy Research, 1985.

American Council on Education. *Fact Book On Higher Education: 1984–85.* Washington, D.C.: American Council on Education, 1984.

Astin, A. W., and others. *The American Freshman: National Norms for Fall 1985*. Washington: American Council on Education, 1985.

Astin, H. S., and Snyder, M. B. "Affirmative Action 1972-1982: A Decade of Response." *Change*, 1982, *59*, 26-31.

Bensimon, E. "Urban Community College Survey." Unpublished manuscript, 1986.

Bers, T. "The Promise and Reality of Women in Community Colleges." Paper presented at American Educational Research Association, Tempe, Arizona, November 1983.

Bowles, S., and Gintis, H. *Schooling in Capitalist America*. New York: Basic Books, 1976.

Cremin, L. *The Transformation of the American School*. New York: Knopf, 1961.

Dziech, B. W. "Changing Status of Women." In G. B. Vaughan and Associates, *Issues for Community College Leaders in a New Era*. San Francisco: Jossey-Bass, 1983.

Fuchs, V. *How We Live*. Cambridge, Mass.: Harvard University Press, 1983.

Gittell, M. "Reaching the Hard to Reach." *Change*, 1985a, *17* (4), 51-60.

Gittell, M. "Women on Welfare: Education and Work." Report to the Ford Foundation, July 1985b.

Hacker, A. "The Decline of Higher Learning." *New York Review of Books*, February 13, 1986, 35-42.

Howe, F. *Myths of Coeducation*. Bloomington: University of Indiana Press, 1984.

Karabel, J. "Community Colleges and Social Stratification: Submerged Class Conflict in American Higher Education." *Harvard Educational Review*, 1972, *42* (4), 521-561.

Ravitch, D. *The Troubled Crusade*. New York: Basic Books, 1983.

Rudolf, F. *The American College and University*. New York: Knopf, 1962.

Touchton, J., and Shavlik, D. *Senior Women Administrators in Higher Education: A Decade of Change, 1975-1983. Preliminary Report*. Washington, D.C.: American Council on Education, 1984.

Marilyn Gittell is professor of political science at the Graduate Center, City University of New York.

Current financial aid practices are diverting funds from traditional-age students to independent adult students.

Independent Students at Two-Year Institutions and the Future of Financial Aid

W. Lee Hansen, Jacob O. Stampen

Despite the existence of a substantial student financial aid system that provides need-based grants, work-study funding, and subsidized loans, we still know relatively little about the impact of this aid on enrollment rates or about the distribution of this aid among different categories of students. The purpose of this chapter is to highlight the distribution of financial aid among students and the various kinds of institutions they attend, paying particular attention to the interplay between being an independent student, being older (age twenty-five and above), receiving need-based student financial aid, and attending community colleges and proprietary schools.

Background

The expansion of need-based student financial aid since the early 1970s has made it easier for students with limited economic resources to enroll and persist in postsecondary education. The provision of grants and work-study funds enables students to pay the costs of their schooling more easily, and the availability of subsidized loans allows them to defer, until after graduation, payment for at least some of their costs of attendance. Dollars allocated to student financial aid rose in real terms (in constant 1982 dollars) from $8.6 billion in 1970-71 to a peak of $17.0 billion in 1980-81 but by 1982-83, the year on which this analysis focuses, declined to $13.0 billion (Gillespie and Carlson, 1983).

The originally assumed purpose of student financial aid programs was to help newly graduating high school students from lower-income families overcome the financial barriers to college attendance. The anticipated effect was to increase enrollments among these young people, thereby augmenting the flow of college-trained individuals into the work force.

Evidence began to accumulate in the early 1980s showing that enrollment rates among young people eighteen to twenty-four did not increase, even though total enrollment did increase. This means that much if not all of the overall enrollment increase must be attributed to the return to school of somewhat older people, those twenty-five and over. The reasons why enrollment of typical college-age youth, and particularly of lower-income youth, failed to increase are unclear, although speculation is rampant: Student financial aid was not abundant enough to exert much effect, aid funds did not keep pace with student costs, family incomes declined in real terms, and so on.

Little more is known about what caused enrollment among older students to increase. Again, there is considerable speculation: Continuing education has become widely accepted among adults; older students are more sensitive to college attendance costs and therefore more responsive to student aid; rapid technological and other changes are requiring ever larger proportions of the experienced labor force to update their training; educational institutions have become more receptive to older students, in light of expected enrollment declines as the eighteen- to twenty-four-year-old cohorts contract through the remainder of the 1980s and into the 1990s.

There is evidence suggesting that older students are more responsive to price than younger students are (Bishop and Van Dyke, 1977). Thus, the greater availability of student financial aid, awarded on the basis of demonstrated financial need, may help to account for the increased enrollment of older people, even if it does not help explain what happened to the traditional college-age population. Whereas need-based student aid has been a continuing presence for typical undergraduates, this has not been the case for older students. Rather, need-based aid has increased in availability as more and more older students have learned that they could qualify for student financial aid through the process of becoming classified as independent. In effect, need-based aid has become a positive incentive, stimulating increased enrollments, and the response of older students to this incentive is not all that surprising, as we shall show later.

More striking is the transformation that has taken place in the goals of student financial aid programs. A review of the development of such programs suggests that they were designed to assist able high school graduates lacking in financial resources to attend postsecondary institutions. But as these programs evolved, it became apparent that older people could qualify for financial aid irrespective of their parents' income, either now or previously (Hansen, 1974). Had they come from higher-income families when they were of typical attendance age, they might not have qualified for aid at the time, but now, on the basis of their low current income, they can qualify for aid.

The possible effects of increasing participation in student financial aid programs are illustrated in Table 1, which includes data from a recent national study of student aid recipients attending public colleges and universities (Stampen, 1985). Here, we see substantial changes occurring in the student aid recipient population over a two-year period. The proportion of aid recipients accounted for by independent students, and particularly nonminority independent students, increased at a rapid rate at the same time that declines occurred among those classified as dependent students. Note especially the sharp decline among dependent minority students. The same study also shows that in 1983–84 nearly 60 percent of the independent aid recipients were twenty-five years old or older. Although the exact cause of these changes cannot be determined on the basis of these figures, it is a fact that aid recipients are increasingly older, independent, nonminority, and married students.

The growing utilization of student financial aid by older students has important effects. Most important, it increases the total demand for student financial aid funds in a period when appropriations, in real dollars, have declined. Also, the increased awarding of aid to older students decreases the size of awards that could be made to younger people. In effect, this development has served to reduce the funding available for recent high school graduates who display financial need and to divert this aid to older people who decide, for whatever reason, to return to school.

Table 1. Distribution of Need-Based Aid Recipients Attending Public Colleges and Universities, 1982–83 and 1983–84, by Dependency and Minority (Ethnic) Status

	Dependent			*Independent*		
	82–83 %	83–84 %	(% Rate of Change)	82–83 %	83–84 %	(% Rate of Change
Minority	20	17	(-15)	12	12	(-0-)
Majority	45	43	(-4)	23	28	(+22)
Total	65	60	(-8)	35	40	(+14)

Source: Stampen, 1985, p. 40.

In the process, student financial aid programs increasingly become programs that provide funds for the continuing education of a potentially wide spectrum of the adult population.

Whether this development is good or bad is not the issue. Rather, it reflects the evolution or transformation of goals that so often occurs with public programs and are not anticipated when the programs are created. As programs begin to serve additional constituencies, they develop new sources of political support, which further solidify the direction in which they are moving. This makes it difficult to know how to evaluate programs. Should they be evaluated in terms of their original or their new goals? It also means that programs slowly change without careful attention to the implications of transformation (Hansen and Lampman, 1974). In particular, old rhetoric often continues to serve as the justification for what has become a quite different program.

Student Aid Programs

We see evidence of this pattern in student financial aid programs. Our interest was first alerted after we discovered the tremendous increase in the numbers and proportions of independent students. By 1984-85, for example, half of all Pell Grant recipients were classified as independent students. This contrasts with a 14 percent figure in 1974-75, just after the Pell Grant program began (Hansen, 1985). The significance of independent student status is that it permits awarding financial aid to students on the basis of their own resources, rather than considering the combined resources of students and their parents. Important tests have been developed to determine who qualifies as independent. Achieving independent status requires the applicant to state on the application form that for the current and prior year he or she has not been claimed as a dependent on the federal income tax form of a parent or guardian, has not received more than $750 from a parent or guardian, and has not lived with a parent or legal guardian for more than six weeks.

These tests have a strong influence on who is likely to qualify as an independent student. Since the tests imply a weakening of the parent-student relationship, older students are much more likely to be independent. Moreover, since older students are more likely to enroll or re-enroll in community colleges or proprietary schools, it seems reasonable to believe that independent student status has opened up enormous possibilities for older students to return to school.

The California Data

Because there are no sufficiently detailed national data bases representing all students (aided as well as nonaided) attending all different kinds of postsecondary institutions benefiting from student aid programs, our analysis employs a 1982-83 data base developed for the state of California. These data reflect the results of a survey of all postsecondary education students in the state, a survey that was designed to shed light on patterns of student expenditures and revenue. Responses were received from 23,000 students, who represent 35 percent of those surveyed. To facilitate the analysis, we confine our attention to full-time students (those taking twelve or more hours of course work per term), who by definition are most likely to receive financial aid.

The underlying data, shown in Table 2, provide the basis for calcu-

Table 2. Distribution of Full-Time Postsecondary Students by Age, Dependent Status, and Receipt of Need-Based Student Financial Aid: All Students and Community College and Proprietary Students, California, 1982-83
(in thousands)

| | Total Students | | | Need-Based Aid Recipients | | |
Age Group	All	Ind.	Dep.	All	Ind.	Dep.
All Students						
Under 22	468	28	440	106	15	92
22-24	134	40	94	31	18	13
25+	171	139	32	50	44	6
Total	773	207	566	188	77	116
Community College Students						
Under 22	195	11	184	20	4	16
22-24	53	18	35	8	7	2
25+	99	83	16	25	22	3
Total	348	112	236	63	32	21
Proprietary School Students						
Under 22	23	3	20	11	2	9
22-24	7	4	3	3	2	1
25+	19	15	4	9	7	2
Total	49	22	27	23	11	12
All Other Postsecondary Students						
Under 22	250	14	236	75	9	67
22-24	74	18	56	20	9	9
25+	53	41	12	16	15	1
Total	376	73	303	102	32	79

Source and Notes: Based on data from the 1982-83 California Student Aid Commission data tape (1985). Students are classified as independent students according to federal rather than California standards.

lating the various percentage figures that are discussed below. We show information for all students, students attending community colleges and proprietary schools, and students attending all other kinds of postsecondary institutions (in this context, the latter include the University of California system, the California State University system, and the private-independent colleges and universities in the state).

What overall patterns emerge from an initial examination of the data?

First, community college and proprietary school students constitute 51 percent of total full-time enrollments in all of California. Community college students alone represent 45 percent of the grand total. This reflects, among other things, the extensive community college system in California.

Second, 32 percent of the community college students and 45 percent of the much smaller group of proprietary school students are classified independent, as compared to 19 percent for all other students. This latter figure hides the considerable diversity that exists among the California State University, the University of California, and the private-independent colleges.

Third, 28 percent of all community college students and 38 percent of all proprietary students are twenty-five and over, as contrasted to 14 percent of all other students. The proportions are substantially lower for the University of California and private-independent systems, which have 7 percent each; 21 percent of CSU system students are twenty-five or older.

This brief review of the evidence makes it quite clear that students at community colleges and proprietary schools are different. They are considerably more likely to be older and independent.

We turn next to information on receipt of need-based student financial aid, discussing the situation first for all students and then focusing on independent students. Among all students in community colleges and proprietary schools, 15 and 48 percent respectively receive need-based student financial aid. The comparable figure for all other students is 27 percent. Aside from differences in the age and independence mix of students, it should be clear that community college students are less likely to qualify and also receive aid, largely because their costs are so small (essentially zero tuition, and neglible living costs for those who commute from home). The situation is quite different for proprietary students, who must pay the full costs of their education; only in this way can they provide owners a reasonable rate of return on their investment. Thus, charges for tuition and books are substantially higher than in public institutions. The other institutions are arrayed between these polar cases; while students do pay tuition, much of the cost of instruction is subsidized by taxpayers.

We now shall consider community college and proprietary students who are twenty-five and older and also independent. We find that 71 percent of older independent students are enrolled in community colleges and proprietary schools. While we have no direct evidence about why older students are so concentrated in these two sectors, some obvious reasons come to mind. For example, both sectors are more likely to offer applied and vocationally oriented coursework, instruction that by its very nature will be more appealing to adults than traditional college-level work. Moreover, students' loss of earnings while in school can be recovered only if the additional schooling enhances the future earning power of the individual.

What do we find when we examine the information on need-based student financial aid? Despite the large number of older independent students, the percentages of them receiving need-based financial aid vary substantially. Among community college students, 27 percent receive need-based aid; among proprietary school students, 47 percent; for all other students, 37 percent. The same cost considerations that were offered earlier apply here to account for differences in overall aid patterns.

While the participation rates do vary, an even more striking fact is that the absolute numbers of older, independent students attending community colleges and proprietary schools exceed those of students attending all other colleges, by a 29 to 15 margin. Put another way, a third of all aid to older independent students goes to those enrolled in what might be called nontraditional institutions.

How does the amount of aid going to older independent students stack up against the overall pattern of need-based aid? Older independent students in community colleges and proprietary schools receive almost 50 percent of the aid going to independent students. Compared to all students receiving need-based aid, however, these students receive only 15 percent of need-based aid.

Questions and Policy Options

Our analysis of the California data helps explain the patterns we observe in the national data, namely, the pronounced increase in the number of Pell Grant recipients who are classified as independent students and their overall replacement of younger dependent students. They receive more aid money and thereby leave less for younger, traditional college-age students. Furthermore, it is clear that much of the recent trend is accounted for by older students attending two-year public and proprietary institutions.

When the student aid programs were first designed, no one thought to differentiate among recipients on the basis of age, because no one expected the rapid growth in the number of older recipients. Now that group is making rapid gains toward displacing the traditional college-age student as the typical aid recipient. It is important to stress, however, that whether older students should receive aid has never been a political issue.

Neither is it likely to become one, since the notion of excluding people because of age is fundamentally foreign to the concept of equity underlying the student financial aid system. Nothing in any of these programs says that student aid is supposed to go to traditional college-age youth. Indeed, the philosophical underpinnings of the Higher Education Amendments of 1972, as voiced by the father of the Pell Grant program, Rhode Island Senator Clayborne Pell, was the belief that every individual in the nation should, if necessary, have the right to a floor of financial support for attending whatever kind of postsecondary institution he or she might choose.

Neither is it possible to contend that students attending one level of postsecondary education are more deserving than those attending another level. The simple fact is that nobody has yet shown that one type of education is more needed by society than another. The nation's political philosophy has consistently seen the role of government as one that facilitates individual initiative, and it is easy to imagne circumstances where it would make as much sense to support the education of a future secretary or policeman as that of a political scientist or physicist. This is particularly evident now, when so many families are headed by women, who often have few possibilities for adequately supporting their dependents other than by obtaining postsecondary education.

Two important problems remain, namely, the growing number of constituencies claiming student financial aid, and the finite resources invested in it. If nontraditional students obtain larger proportions of student aid, others must obtain less. We fear it is the eighteen- to twenty-four-year-olds who are losing out, the very group for whom student financial aid was originally intended. This group also includes large proportions of students from economically disadvantaged minority groups. The problem is aggravated by several proposals before the U.S. Congress. In essence, these substitute age as the major criterion for determining independent student status and eligibility to receive financial aid. This represents a sharp departure from current rules, which consider low income to be the primary criterion to consider in the awarding of financial aid. Under these new rules, more students would be eligible to receive aid, and more would be likely to apply (Gladieux, 1985). Students moving from dependent to independent status would also be eligible to receive larger grants. Since total dollars invested in student aid are diminishing, however, across-the-board reductions are likely. Thus, it seems clear that younger dependent students in need of financial assistance will have greater difficulty in the future obtaining the resources they need (Hansen, Reeves, and Stampen, 1985).

The problem with the current requirements is that they are difficult to monitor and enforce. Indeed, the primary motivation for the proposed changes is to simplify the existing standards and make them more enforceable. For example, under the existing standards, beyond verifying that parents do not claim their children as tax dependents, how can policy makers know that a student in a given year received only $750 dollars from a parent or lived with them for only six weeks? Nevertheless, the existing standards do make the purpose of student financial aid programs quite clear: to serve the needs of students who genuinely lack the resources to finance postsecondary education.

This fact also points toward at least a partial solution to the problem, that is, to learn more about independent students and develop better ways of evaluating their claims for financial assistance. This important element was overlooked when the current programs were formed. Ever since, student aid officers have had difficulty comparing the needs of dependent and independent students in order to determine which individuals are more deserving than others. This also shows that the rapid growth in the proportion of aid recipients both above traditional college age and independent was completely unanticipated by policy makers.

In the short run, we recommend retention of the previous standards, which determine eligibility for aid on the basis of financial need. In the long run, we need to accelerate research leading to better ways of assessing the needs of dependent and independent students. The current trend endangers the future of student aid in that it promises to dilute existing resources to the point where effectiveness can no longer be expected.

References

Bishop, J., and Van Dyke, J. "Can Adults be Hooked on College? Some Determinants of Adult College Attendance." *Journal of Higher Education*, 1977, *12* (1), 40-59.

Gillespie, D., and Carlson, N. *Trends in Student Financial Aid, 1963 to 1983*. Washington, D.C.: The Washington Office of the College Board, 1983.

Gladieux, L. "An Improved Definition of Independent Student Status under Federal Aid Programs." Testimony before the Subcommittee on Postsecondary Education, Committee on Education and Labor, U.S. House of Representatives, August 1, 1985.

Hansen, W. L. "The Financial Implications of Student Independence." In *Who Pays? Who Benefits? A National Invitational Conference on the Independent Student*. New York: The College Examination Board, 1974.

Hansen, W. L. *The Growth of Independent Students and the Incentive to Become Independent*. Program Report 85-12. Madison: Wisconsin Center for Education Research, 1985.

Hansen, W. L., and Lampman, R. J. "Basic Opportunity Grants for Higher Education: Will the Outcome Differ from the Intent?" *Challenge*, 1974, November/December, 46-51.

Hansen, W. L., Reeves, R., and Stampen, J. *The Implications of Redefining the Independent Student*. Program Report 85-10. Madison: Wisconsin Center for Education Research, 1985.

Stampen, J. *Student Aid and Public Higher Education: Recent Changes*. Washington, D.C.: American Association of State Colleges and Universities, 1985.

W. Lee Hansen has written extensively on the costs, benefits, and financing of higher education. Jacob O. Stampen is a higher education policy analyst and planner and has authored studies and data bases pertaining to student aid, governance, and finance. Both are members of the National Institute of Education–financed National Center for Postsecondary Governance and Finance. They are at the University of Wisconsin in Madison.

Community college students who are the first in their families to find their way into higher education face distinctive problems, both on campus and at home. Their difficulties are related to the social role of the community college.

Strangers to Our Shores

Howard B. London

The purpose of this volume is to rejoin a now-lapsed debate—most vigorous in the 1960s and 1970s—between advocates and critics of the American community college. That debate was, of course, part of a larger national struggle over the kind of society we were and aspired to be. As such, it questioned not just education (at all levels) but also the workings of government, the economy, religion, the family, and our society at large. In its barest form, the educational debate concerned whether schools fostered equality or inequality of opportunity. Questions of why, how, and to what extent they did gave rise to a voluminous and oftentimes contradictory literature of research and social commentary.

In the debate over community colleges, advocates pointed to the successes of both liberal arts and vocational curricula, especially for nontraditional students—working-class, minority, and older students—who in previous generations were unlikely to find themselves in college. From this point of view, community colleges were seen as promoting opportunities for upward mobility for able and diligent students, regardless of background. Critics, in contrast, saw community colleges as helping to perpetuate an unfair status quo by preventing or minimizing the upward

---

I am indebted to Helen Reinherz of the Simmons College Graduate School of Social Work and to Barbara S. Spivak for their contributions to this manuscript, and to Sophie Freud for bringing Helm Stierlin's work to my attention.

mobility of mostly lower-status students. They pointed to the dwindling proportion of community college liberal arts graduates and to evidence that the chief opportunity for those students, liberal arts and vocational majors alike, was to maintain their relative socioeconomic status in the face of a changing occupational structure. Like a long column of soldiers stepping out at once, community college students were pictured as never moving any closer to the people in the middle or front ranks: at best (and this was not even always the case), they were destined to join the lower echelons of the new white-collar proletariat. Thus, the former view was meritocratic, with the community college holding out the promise of the American dream. In the latter view, the promise was a false one, the dream an insidious illusion. (For purposes of contrast, these themes are drawn here in bold relief. There were, of course, elaborations and variations.)

My own contribution to that debate (London, 1978) was an ethnography based on one year of participant observation and on dozens of interviews at an urban, white, working-class community college. The students were described as having a profound belief in an ethic of individualism, a generally accepted view in our culture, which told them that personal achievement was a matter of intelligence, diligence, and self-control. Some of the more poignant statements were from students attributing their lot in life thus far, including their poor academic histories, to a self-perceived lack of these traits. In the face of these self-doubts, many students were nevertheless attempting to leave their blue-collar communities by way of the college.

As they discovered, however, a graceful leave taking was not always possible, since it usually required a painful and anxious renegotiation of relationships with family, friends, and even with themselves. For some students, the very act of enrolling in a liberal arts curriculum was a statement of white-collar aspirations and thus a signal—especially to others, who were not going on—that old ties were now suspect. To then do poorly in school was therefore particularly disappointing and embarassing. To do very well, however, called for changes in relationships, life-styles (with more time devoted to school work), and self-conceptions that could also be distressing. Both failure and success, then, left many students vulnerable, and this double bind helped explain the presence in the student culture of mores against academic achievement, or at least against doing too well too soon:

> There is always a price to be paid for emancipation, and in cases like this, those who make the move feel ambivalent about their success in school. They have been told of the virtues and dividends of educational achievement, yet they cannot feel completely comfortable with it. . . . If a transition was to be made in their lives, it would occur slowly.

Having done poorly in high school, it is not surprising that, still in their own city and still with old friends, they would proceed tentatively and cautiously. . . . [T]hey were hedging against the possibility of failure, yet they were also cushioning themselves from the social-psychological consequences of success, of becoming "middle class" (London, 1978, p. 103).

The London (1978) study offered a critical view of the community college and by implication of society itself, pointing as it did to the deterrents encountered by working-class students and to a social system that unduly dampens potentialities and, intentionally or not, wastes talent. For present purposes, however, it is important to recall that the study also chronicled "negative cases," that is, subcultures (mostly of older students) who were quite enthusiastic not just about upward mobility but also about broadening their horizons. They wanted not just a job, but a view about jobs. They wanted not so much to live the good life as to live a good life. They almost always found a teacher or were found by a teacher with whom they developed a special relationship. Outside the constraining, normative system of the mainstream student culture, they were, in a sense, strangers in paradise.

Students Who Beat the Odds

There was no follow-up study of these or other students. Furthermore, the study was of the college's first year of operation, so that there were no statistics on previous classes nor any lore built up among students about the successes or failures of their predecessors. To the extent that it supported the community college critics, the study did so by examining how the culture of one institution contributed to the muting of aspirations. But what, then, to make of the "negative cases"—an ironic term— in which the college contributed to the meeting of aspirations? Depending on one's viewpoint, such cases may or may not challenge the overall assessment of community colleges having played a conservative social role; at the very least, however, these cases demonstrate that community colleges, like most other institutions, can play diverse and sometimes contradictory roles for different groups of people. Any full analysis is obligated to acknowledge and examine these roles as well.

In one such analysis, Neumann and Riesman (1980) interviewed blue-collar community college students who transferred to selective independent four-year institutions. In accounting for their successes, students credited an aggregate of factors: initial academic success, increased participation in college life, student support groups, and special attention and positive reinforcement from respected faculty who recognized their superior work. The authors concluded that the fortune of these students "involves a complex of social and psychological factors converging at critical points in the educational career" (p. 70).

Because Neumann and Riesman took educational histories only, it is not surprising that students cited in-school factors. In an effort to discern whether any outside influences come into play, in my recent research I have collected family and social as well as educational histories. Participating in the study are students who are the first in their families of origin ever to have gone to college, whether to two- or four-year institutions. Their parents, brothers, and sisters had no higher education. By all conventional standards, they are from working- or lower-class homes. Like those described by Neumann and Riesman, the students described here have all transferred from community colleges to four-year liberal arts institutions.

Focusing on students who have beaten the odds may be taken by community college advocates as an implicit endorsement, even a celebration, of the meritocratic view. Then again, the great difficulties (described below) experienced by these students, to say nothing of the problems of those who have not gone so far, may be taken as supporting the critics' view. I believe the weight of evidence supports this latter view at the same time that it serves as a caution against narrowly based class theorems of the role of the community college. That said, the following is offered as a brief overview of only part of the research still in progress.

Thirteen students from a variety of Greater Boston colleges, from blue-collar to elite, have been interviewed so far. The tape-recorded sessions range from one to seven hours, depending on the responsiveness of individual students. Because lists of first-generational students (as I call them) are not kept by colleges, recruitment notices were posted in dormitories and other campus buildings, ads were placed in college newspapers, contacts were made through friends, and in one case there was a chance meeting. The sample is neither scientific nor reprensentative (although students of both sexes and various racial and ethnic groups are included), but the findings may still be suggestive and worth knowing.

Family Dynamics and Matriculation

An Overview of the Literature. The expansion of two- and four-year colleges and the arrival on campus of nontraditional students has been attributed to many interrelated social factors: changes in technology, increasingly sophisticated jobs that require ever more education, an escalation of educational credentialism, competition among groups for social status, mollification of the educationally disenfranchised, and so on. Whatever the reasons for this expansion, not everyone has been affected equally. Indeed, there is an extensive literature on the sources of unequal educational achievement. Among the variables investigated are the socioeconomic composition of a high school's student body, family socioeconomic status, parental encouragement, school climate, school quality, the financial resources of the school, teacher expectations, sociolinguistic styles, and peer and reference groups.

Although there is little in the literature on the role of family dynamics, it is precisely to them that first-generation students have pointed as an important propelling force in their lives. In a pioneering study by Kahl (1953), college-bound working-class males reported that their fathers, disappointed with their own life accomplishments, had been emphasizing the value of education for many years. The fathers, then, were especially significant to their sons' educational plans. By contrast, Ellis and Lane (1963) found that among lower-strata Stanford University students the mother was most influential, especially if her educational and occupational attainments outranked those of her husband. We shall return to these studies later.

Parental Delegations. As students discussed family life, it gradually became apparent that, in effect, they were delegated by parents to carry out distinctive tasks or missions. These delegations, as described below, met some strong parental needs at the same time that they helped mold their children's educational aspirations. Here, the psychoanalytic thought of Stierlin (1974) has been most helpful. Stierlin focuses on individuation and separation between parents and adolescents. Elemental issues are brought into play: "losing and refinding what one holds dearest, deepest distress and joy, conflict and reconciliation . . . the nature of love, of obedience, and of mutual growth and liberation in families" (pp. ix-x). In the context of such issues, the adolescent delegate "may move out of the parental orbit but remains tied to his parents by the long leash of loyalty. This delegate must then fulfill missions for his parents . . . that [may] embroil him in various forms of conflict" (pp. xii-xiii). Dictated by the emotional needs of parents, a mission thus consists of both a "sending out" and a "holding on."

Listening and relistening to the tapes of my interviews, I was struck by how casually students discussed these missions, as though they were taken for granted, part of the fabric of the family tapestry. One student talked at length of his father's oft-repeated lament that his own career had gone sour and of how his father connected this to his wishes for the son:

> All my life I heard that story of how things, if they had gone differently and if he hadn't . . . made bad moves [decisions], . . . would have been . . . different, better. "So study, go to a good college *so I can feel like I did something*" (emphasis added).

The father was depicted as beseeching the son to provide him with a sense of completeness ("So I can feel like I did something"). "Do this for me," he seems to be saying, "so I won't have to feel so bad about myself." On his part, the student has played the attendant son, obeying the entreaties by always having done well in school.

In another example, a young woman described how her mother spoke of her own parents' great displeasure at the mother's choice of a husband:

> She [the student's mother] said they thought she could do better. It wasn't [that she was a] Protestant [a fifth-generation German-American family] and he was a Catholic [a second-generation Irish-American] but [that] he didn't have enough school and he wouldn't amount to much.

This student was born two years after the marriage. Five years later, the stormy marriage ended. Later in the interview, when discussing how her mother (with whom she lived) encouraged her educationally, she stated:

> She said if I really did well in school *she wouldn't feel so crummy*, that she had got me off to a bad start, and that her folks were maybe right [about the husband], but she could still point to me in college.

The mission here seems to take the form of the mother saying (to herself, her parents, her daughter, and perhaps to the ex-husband), "You see, if my daughter is in college, then things didn't turn out so badly after all. I can in this way be relieved from at least some of my guilt, fears, and failures. I don't have to feel so crummy."

We are left to wonder whether the disappointed fathers in Kahl's (1953) research and the "downwardly married" mothers in Ellis and Lane's (1963) were playing out similar dramas. Stierlin claims that parents often use their children for their own emotional needs. This can be damaging if, for example, children come to be so weighted down by the parents' unmet aspirations and unresolved conflicts that they follow the parents' wishes at the expense of becoming persons in their own right. Imprisoned by loyalty, they forfeit their own autonomy. The delegation of a mission, however, can also be personally and socially beneficial. It "often is the expression of a necessary and legitimate process of a relationship. Delegation gives our lives direction and significance; it is the sheer anchor of obligations reaching down through the generations" (Stierlin, 1974, p. 23).

Indeed, it would be too facile and distorting to conclude that parental delegations alone compelled these students to achieve, or that they are utterly bound to their parents. The situation is more complicated than that. To fulfill their missions, students must leave the parental orbit, the leaving itself thus paradoxically becoming a sign of allegiance (as stated previously, the process requires both a "sending out" and a "holding on"). Potentially, this can lead to considerable conflict, as when students find themselves juggling and keeping separate (rather than integrating) the parts of themselves that are staying and leaving.

Juggling Two Worlds

Nowhere is this juggling better seen than in students' accounts of their difficulties in bridging the worlds of the home and the campus. According to one community college student, who later transferred to a prestigious four-year college:

> One day at home I used the word "nefarious." My father says, "Oh, the college boy's home." I said something like, "You know what it means?" He says, "No, big shot. Tell me." So I told him, and he says, "That's my boy," but I couldn't tell if he was angry or what. The next time I used a word like that he said, "Jesus Christ," and sits there shaking his head. I thought he was angry. About what? About me going to. . . . being different . . . than I was. I was careful after, . . . at home, how I spoke.

Self-preservation on campus was also problematic, especially during the first semester. Whether at community colleges or four-year colleges, the first-generation students interviewed felt out of place, sometimes intensely so. Reported one community college student:

> I remember trying to stay away from the cafeteria because it was just so wide open. I felt . . . that the minute I walked through, everybody would look at me, or whoever was right in that area anyway. . . . You don't know what to do. . . . I mean, I don't belong here, who am I kidding? This is ridiculous. Even though it was a community college, it still looked like they [the other students] were from a different place. That was probably my own little problem, but that's still what it looked like.

In an ironic way, she was right; it was her "own little problem" in that the class culture of most of the other students was the same as her own, as she later learned. It was in large part her fear of being different that initially led her to manufacture differences. For students like her, then (including four-year college students), the campus was a world of appearances; initially, at least, they became intensely concerned with socially "passing." Without detailing them here, impressions were managed around such things as vocabulary, accent, conversational topics, clothing, and, for one student, the inner decor of his car.

These data suggest certain connections between identity, education, and society. To be accepted as a full member of a status group and to share with others a sense of membership in it, regardless of its prestige or power, requires socialization into its culture: its styles of language, dress, aesthetic tastes, values, manners, conversational topics, and preferences in sports, media, and the arts (Collins, 1971). Indeed, Weber (1968) argued that the chief social function of education was to provide and certify socialization into the culture of a social class. For middle-class students on middle-class campuses, it is mostly further socialization, more steps in a continuous process. For first-generation students, it is a resocialization, a jarring point of departure. At home, however, they tried, for a while at least, to remain the same. From their point of view, the learning of academic and job-related skills and knowledge was important, but what mattered most in their day-to-day lives in both worlds, especially during the first year, were matters of style. Thus, the putting on of the new student role was tentative, and its attendant performances were precisely what separated students from the past and from the people who still inhabited it. These, then, are some of the additional hurdles faced by first-generation students.

Cautions and Disclaimers

First, it should not be assumed that all or most first-generation students, even the ones cited here, are motivated only by the concerns described above. In the full interviews, the students gave any number of reasons for matriculation—vocational and professional aspirations, intellectual fulfillment, and so on—that are part of what probably is an ever shifting hierarchy of motives. To see these students as driven only by the forces of family dynamics is too unidimensional an approach. To omit these forces from consideration, however, is to miss something of importance.

Second, as previously noted, the sample was a self-selected one. These students may or may not have been the most eager to talk of family matters; others may have been either too eager or not eager enough to do so. Thus, the students cited here may not be representative of any group, and how many first-generation students are at all like them has not been established.

Third, the experiences of first-generation students can be exciting. There was much talk in the interviews, talk not reported here, of scales falling from the eyes and of new vistas and possibilities. To focus on the difficulties is not to deny the joys and the precious rewards.

This chapter began by contrasting two views of the American community college: one a more meritocratic, laudatory, and conservative view, the other more critical and radical. Psychologizing, as I have done, may itself be taken as a turn toward that more conservative view, especially given our culture's penchant for seeing individuals as responsible for their own fates, as if fate were unaffected by social context. However, by adding psychodynamic formulations and connecting them to sociological concepts of social class, socialization, and culture, we acquire, I believe, a better-rounded view of society's machinations. Indeed, one can argue that the sons and daughters of middle-class families can also be in the emotional and social employ of their parents. What distinguishes the odyssey of these working-class, first-generation students is that their journey takes them into what can be experienced as an alien land. No account of inequality, of educational success or failure, or of upward mobility (whether psychodynamically or sociologically based) can ignore that their distinctive struggles are related to their being strangers to our shores.

References

Collins, R. "Functional and Conflict Theories of Educational Stratification." *American Sociological Review*, 1971, *36*, 1002-1019.

Ellis, R., and Lane, W. "Structural Supports for Upward Mobility." *American Sociological Review*, 1963, *28*, 743-756.

Kahl, J. "Educational and Occupational Aspirations of Common-Man Boys." *Harvard Educational Review*, 1953, *23*, 186-203.

London, H. *The Culture of Community College.* New York: Praeger, 1978.

Neumann, W., and Riesman, D. "The Community College Elite." In G. B. Vaughan (Ed.), *Questioning the Community College Role.* New Directions for Community Colleges, no. 32. San Francisco: Jossey-Bass, 1980.

Stierlin, H. *Separating Parents and Adolescents.* New York: Quadrangle, 1974.

Weber, M. *Economy and Society.* New York: Bedminster, 1968.

Howard B. London is associate professor of sociology at Bridgewater State College and author of The Culture of Community College.

This chapter draws from the ERIC (Educational Resources Information Center) data base to provide further sources of information on the social role of the community college.

Sources and Information: The Social Role of the Community College

Jim Palmer

The preceding chapters in this sourcebook raise serious questions regarding the social role of the community college, charging that two-year institutions have done little to raise the socioeconomic status of minorities and the poor. This concluding chapter draws from materials in the ERIC data base to review additional writings on related themes: community colleges as stepping-stones to the baccalaureate, college efforts to improve transfer rates, college efforts to assist minorities and women, and the community college share of student financial aid.

Community Colleges as Stepping-Stones to the Baccalaureate

How many community college students transfer to four-year institutions and then go on to earn the baccalaureate? Given the importance of the baccalaureate as a credential in the labor market, no question is more important to those studying the college impact on student social mobility. Yet accurate data on student transfers are not readily available. Cohen (1979) points out that methods of counting transfer students vary greatly from state to state and that while most studies define transfer students as

L. S. Zwerling (Ed.). *The Community College and Its Critics.*
New Directions for Community Colleges, no. 54. San Francisco: Jossey-Bass, June 1986.
101

those who have taken courses at a community college and subsequently enroll at a senior institution, there is little agreement among the states as to the number of units that must be taken before the student achieves transfer status. Cohen also points out that data obtained by college-based researchers are frequently invalidated by low response rates to surveys. And, in cases where the community colleges rely exclusively on surrounding universities for transfer information, figures may be particularly misleading due to incomplete data and other imbalances caused by varying data collection methods.

Student follow-up studies in the ERIC data base confirm these statistical limitations. Most colleges survey only their graduates and have scant information on the further education of students who leave without earning an associate degree. These graduate surveys usually achieve only modest response rates, and because they are conducted only once (usually between six and twelve months after graduation), they provide no information on the educational progress of students who earn an associate degree, drop out of college for a year or two, and then enroll in a baccalaureate-granting institution. Davis and others (1985), for example, conducted a survey in the fall of 1984 of those students who had graduated from Sinclair Community College (Ohio) earlier in the year. The survey solicited information on the graduates' characteristics, on their perceptions of college services, and on their current activities. Fifty-two percent of the graduates provided usable responses. In another survey designed to measure job placement and transfer rates of students graduating from Broome Community College (New York), Scott (1985) achieved a 93 percent response rate, but the bulk of the data was collected in person during graduation rehearsal. Other examples of graduate surveys that provide information on the continuing education of students include Friedlander (1985), McMaster (1985), John Tyler Community College (1985), Nienkamp (1984), and Weintraub (1984).

In order to avoid the limitations of these graduate surveys, some colleges have attempted to measure the success of their transfer programs by collecting data on former students who are enrolled in surrounding baccalaureate-granting institutions. Johnson County Community College (JCCC) in Kansas, for example, identified and surveyed 1,100 of its former students (graduates and nongraduates) who were enrolled at the University of Kansas during the fall of 1983. At the same time, JCCC also surveyed a control group of 1,100 native University of Kansas students and compared findings on the basis of demographic characteristics and educational experiences (Johnson County Community College, 1984). Other colleges— including Nassau Community College (New York), the Community College of Philadelphia (Pennsylvania), and Los Rios Community College District (California)—have used transcript data supplied by surrounding colleges and universities to examine the academic success of former students who have transferred to baccalaureate-granting institutions (Fernandez and others, 1984; Renkiewicz, 1985; Community College of Philadelphia, 1982, 1984). By identifying those senior institutions that receive the majority of their transfer students, two-year colleges can secure the cooperation of those senior institutions in efforts to track the academic progress of community college transfers. Nonetheless, these efforts are hampered by the varying data collection procedures used by senior institutions. Researchers at the Community College of Philadelphia, for example, found that "although all schools list the courses the students take internally, this is where the standardization ends" (Community College of Philadelphia, 1984, p. 2).

The most comprehensive data on community college transfers, however, have indeed been collected with the cooperation of senior institutions. The Illinois Community College Board, for example, has been gathering data from public and private baccalaureate-granting institutions from across the state in a longitudinal study of the persistence and graduation rates of 10,015 students who transferred to those senior institutions from Illinois two-year colleges in the fall of 1979 (Bragg, 1982a, 1982b, 1982c; Illinois Community College Board, 1984). In another longitudinal study, Richardson and Doucette (1980) compared the academic persistence, performance, and degree attainment of native students and community college transfer students at three Arizona universities: Arizona State University, the University of Arizona, and Northern Arizona University. Other statewide comparisons of community college transfer students and native university students have been conducted in Florida (Florida State Department of Education, 1983) and in Kansas (Doucette and Teeter, 1985; Johnson County Community College, 1985). All of these studies indicate that overall persistence and graduation rates for community college transfers are lower than the persistence and graduation rates of native university students. The data from Illinois and Arizona, however, suggest that community college students who transfer with an associate degree or with at least two years of study at the community college perform better at the senior institution than those who do not earn an associate degree or those who transfer with less than two years of study at the community college.

But even with the cooperation of senior institutions in providing accurate data on community college transfers, analysts are still faced with the problem of calculating an accurate transfer rate to gauge the percentage of potential community college transfer students who do indeed transfer. Determining the number of potential transfer students who are enrolled in community colleges has been the major stumbling block in calculating transfer rates. In California these rates can range greatly depending on the enrollment measure used to identify potential transfers. If total headcount enrollment is used, then the transfer rate is 3 percent. If the number of full-time, college-age students is used, then the transfer rate is

17 percent. If the number of first-time, full-time college-age students is used, the transfer rate jumps to 59 percent. And, if potential transfer students are defined as the number of first-time, full-time students who *intend* to transfer, then the transfer rate is 71 percent (California Community Colleges, 1984, p. 14). Community college leaders have complained that reports of low transfer rates are flawed by improper calculations of the number of potential transfers. Heinselman (1985) recommends that transfer rates be calculated as the ratio of students transferring in the fall to the number of sophomores enrolled in the college during the previous fall semester. McCabe (1984) argues that two-year colleges should develop a realistic process of evaluating the transfer function by excluding from computation those students who do not intend to complete an associate degree program. Cohen and others (1985), however, present evidence indicating that the self-reported degree aspirations of community college students may not be accurate discriminators of transfer potential.

Facilitating Transfer

Data limitations notwithstanding, several community colleges have undertaken efforts to assess the transfer function and to improve the chances that all who aspire to the baccalaureate will achieve it. Recent studies commissioned in California have called for a renewed emphasis on the transfer function, especially in light of the disproportionately large number of minority students who depend on the colleges as a port of entry to the university. Weiler and others (1985) argue that educational leaders in California need to address at least three problems facing the transfer function: (1) low minority transfer rates, a problem exacerbated by limited counseling services, student financial problems, and the lingering belief that minority students naturally gravitate toward vocational education; (2) lower academic course standards that make it difficult for community college transfers to compete at the university; and (3) inadequate program articulation and coordination between the community colleges and the state's public four-year colleges and universities. In light of these and other concerns, the California State Postsecondary Education Commission (1985) outlines several recommendations for improving the transfer function. These recommendations are far-ranging, dealing with (1) methods of improving the high school preparation of transfer students; (2) the need to identify, assess, and counsel potential transfer students; (3) the need to strengthen the quality and depth of the community college collegiate curriculum; (4) methods of providing students with adequate information on transferring; and (5) the need for improved coordination and planning among all segments of higher education in the state. These recommendations underscore the fact that efforts to enhance transferring involve an array of activities, including counseling, curriculum development, and intersegmental articulation and cooperation.

Projects undertaken by twenty-four community colleges participating in the Ford Foundation's Urban Community College Transfer Opportunities Program (UCCTOP) illustrate the range of these activities. Cohen and others (1985) summarize these activities, noting that they encompass course and curriculum devlopment, student recruitment, interinstitutional articulation, the involvement of alumni as role models, special activities for minority students, assessment and placement activities, and tutorial and counseling services. J. Sargeant Reynolds Community College (Virginia), for example, used alumni volunteers in an outreach project that encouraged inner-city high school students to plan and complete a baccalaureate education (J. Sargeant Reynolds Community College, 1984). Laney College (California) encouraged study groups, workshops, and transfer seminars to help students meet their transfer goals (Shimabukuro, 1984). In another example, Honolulu Community College (Hawaii) worked on the development of a conceptual design for a student tracking system (Honolulu Community College, 1984). The actual impact of these and other UCCTOP projects on student success in transferring is hard to judge. But the projects have at least underscored the colleges' commitment to transfer and to the importance of helping students achieve the baccalaureate. Several ERIC documents provide additional information on the UCCTOP activities: Compton Community College, 1984; Dunn and Greb, 1984; Fonseca, 1984; Highland Park Community College, 1984; Houston Community College System, 1984; McGrath, 1984; Polowczyk, 1984; Sacramento City College, 1984; San Diego City College, 1984; Sotiriou and Ireland, 1984; and West Los Angeles College, 1984.

Assisting Minority Students

Issues related to student transfer are closely conncected to issues surrounding the community college role in promoting the educational and occupational mobility of minority students. Because minorities are overrepresented in community colleges (Olivas, 1979; Katsinas, 1984), two-year institutions are an extremely important link in efforts to increase minority attainment of baccalaureate and higher degrees. The California State Postsecondary Education Commission (1985), for example, declares that the state's affirmative action goals for higher education are highly dependent on the community colleges. The success of the community colleges in carrying out this affirmative action role is, to say the least, a point of great debate in the literature.

Many writers argue that community college responses to minority students are inadequate and that much more needs to be done before minority students achieve parity in higher education. Garza (1984) notes the small number of Hispanic faculty members at community colleges and argues that more Hispanic instructors and administrators need to be hired so that the growing number of Hispanic students will find on-campus role models. Cain (1982) takes a similar approach, making the point that the conservative backgrounds and attitudes of most community college faculty thwart the development of innovative programs required to provide equal educational opportunity to the large numbers of nontraditional students entering community colleges. Turning to pedagogical issues, Roueche (1981) contends that open admissions policies will not secure the success of nontraditional students (many of whom are minorities) until colleges adopt "mastery learning" and other innovative instructional techniques designed to help students overcome prior learning deficiencies. And in a study of higher education opportunities in Chicago, Orfield and others (1984) maintain that community colleges are part of a second-class educational track that begins at the elementary level. Students from minority neighborhoods, the authors argue, are tracked into community colleges rather than four-year institutions, and those minority students who do transfer are more likely to end up at less-prestigious baccalaureate-granting colleges. Thus, community colleges are often seen in the literature as failing in their obligations to minority students, especially in the areas of providing role models, appropriate instruction, and—in the final analysis—opportunities for educational advancement.

Other authors, however, point out the difficult and mitigating circumstances under which community colleges work to assist minorities. Cohen (1984), for example, notes that Hispanic students have relatively poor academic records at all levels of education and that it is inappropriate to single out community colleges as doing a disservice to these students. Indeed, educational difficulties of many minority students begin long before college matriculation. Hayward (1985) argues that low transfer rates among Hispanic and black students have their roots in the record of failure that many of the students suffer in high school. Disproportionately large numbers of these students drop out before reaching the twelfth grade, he points out, and of those students who do receive a high school diploma, relatively few are eligible to enter the University of California or the California State University System. Hayward concludes that "when these lamentable graduation and eligibility rates are related to actual participation rates in community colleges and the four-year segments there is little wonder that the transfer rate of black and Hispanic students continues to lag behind those of other students" (p. 5). Other authors, including Woodland and Goldstein (1984) and Samuels (1985) also point to the poor academic performance of minorities in high school and call on colleges to begin their recruitment and intervention efforts before minority students matriculate. Minority students, these writers point out, are often tracked out of the academic curriculum before high school graduation, thus handicapping the students before they enter the community college.

Relatively few examples of college assistance to minorities at the high school level are presented in the literature. Some of the UCCTOP activities mentioned above do involve college efforts to inform minority high school students of their opportunities for a baccalaureate education (J. Sargeant Reynolds Community College, 1984). Harris and Rohfeld (1983) describe a program undertaken by Cuyahoga Community College (Ohio) to help improve the test-taking skills of inner-city high school students and to help them build the skills needed to succeed in postsecondary education. Most of the literature, though, focuses on efforts to help minorities once they are at the college. These efforts include the Mathematics Intervention Project initiated by the Border College Consortium to increase Hispanic participation in mathematics instruction (Rendon, 1983); the career-planning curriculum designed at San Jose City College (California) for Chicano or Latino students (Douglas and others, 1982); the minority advising program for black students at Gainesville Junior College in Georgia (Seerley and Webb, 1985); and the black advisory committee established at Valencia Community College (Florida) to monitor and assess the progress made by the college in increasing the enrollment and meeting the needs of black students (Valencia Community College, 1980).

The Community College Role in Promoting the Social Status of Women

In comparison to issues surrounding the college role in promoting transfer and assisting minorities, relatively little has been written about the college role in assisting women. Dzierlenga (1981) presents a comprehensive review of this literature through 1980. Since then, authors writing about women at the community college—like authors dealing with minorities and transfers—argue that the colleges have not done enough to promote social equity. Bers (1983) maintains that "the promise of comprehensive and appropriate support services, an egalitarian academic world, and well-paying nontraditional careers for many has not been realized" (p. 17). She also argues that societal norms and economic realities are to blame, as well as "old fashioned sexism" (p. 32).

In light of these unmet needs, the literature calls on colleges to provide special support services for women, especially for older, returning women students and for women entering nontraditional occupational fields that are dominated by men. Osterkamp and Hullett (1983) marshal demographic and economic data to underscore the need for a women's reentry program at Bakersfield College (California) that would focus on recruitment, orientation, advising, admissions assistance, counseling, career development, child care, financial aid, and job placement. A wide variety of services is also suggested by Wintersteen (1982), whose survey of returning women at North Shore Community College (Massachusetts) resulted in a series of recommendations concerning recruitment and retention, career and vocational counseling, social support services, and credit for prior learning. Herman and others

(1984) focus on nontraditional occupations and describe the Women in Technology program at Corning Community College (New York). The program utilizes volunteers to (1) address the stereotyping that discourages women from entering technological programs, (2) examine sexist attitudes and instructional materials, (3) sensitize faculty to the messages they transmit to women in technological fields, and (4) provide support services for women in a male-dominated classroom.

While most support services for women focus on the needs of enrolled students, at least one document describes a college initiative to assist women in the population at large. McWilliams (1982) details the components of the Barrier Reduction Program for Women operated by Cedar Valley College (Texas). The program—an offshoot of the college's perceived "obligation to meet the multiple needs of the mature women of South Dallas County" (p. 3)—offers workshops and individual career consultations to help area women meet their personal needs, increase their knowledge of career opportunities, and realize their individual potential. Included in the program are weekend workshops on resume writing, job interviewing, assertiveness training, and women's legal rights; seminars on self-esteem and career options investigation; and other events such as discussion groups and documentary film presentations. The program, in effect, is a community services effort.

Student Financial Aid

A final issue having an effect on the college role in promoting educational and social mobility is the question of whether or not two-year college students receive their fair share of student financial aid. The literature on this subject leans to the conclusion that community college students do not receive an equitable share of financial aid and that the colleges have not been aggressive enough in correcting this situation. Gladieux (1975) argues that application, allotment, and allocation procedures do not inherently mitigate against the participation of two-year colleges in federal student assistance programs, but that many community colleges simply do not apply for the funds. Peng (1979) agrees, noting that funds going to two-year colleges have not increased in proportion to their enrollment and that many colleges during the 1970s simply did not apply for one or more of the campus-based programs. As to the question of why the colleges do not apply, Nelson (1976), Russo (1976), and Johnson (1982) argue that the image of the two-year college as a low-cost institution has resulted in the general tendency to ignore the nontuition costs of attending college and to consequently place little priority in developing strong financial aid offices.

It should be noted, however, that many of these works are written from the perspective of the 1970s and may not accurately describe financial aid practices as they exist today. Furthermore, some authors caution that debates concerning the equitable distribution of student financial aid are clouded by insufficient data and by muddled conceptual issues such as conflicting opinions about how to define student need. Nelson (1980) concludes that there are grounds for concern about the underutilization of aid by community colleges, but that there is no standard against which the equity of student aid distribution can be judged. She also argues that "even if a standard is rationally selected, the lack of necessary data prevents the standard from being satisfactorily compared with the actual aid distributions" (p. 39). Hyde and Augenblick (1980) make similar arguments, noting the difficulties encountered in defining and measuring an institution's "fair share" as well as the problems imposed by the dearth of empirical data on the distribution of financial aid to community college students. Determining whether community college students receive their fair share of financial aid is not a matter of simple arithmetic.

Conclusion

This chapter has reviewed a selection of the available ERIC literature on only four of the many issues surrounding the community college role in promoting equity and social mobility. Further citations can be obtained through computer or manual searches of ERIC's *Resources in Education* (RIE) and *Current Index to Journals in Education* (CIJE).

Most of those citations listed in the references section below are ERIC documents (marked with an "ED" number) and can be ordered through the ERIC Document Reproduction Service (EDRS) in Alexandria, Virginia, or obtained on microfiche at 650 libraries across the country. For an EDRS order form and/or a list of the libraries in your state that have ERIC microfiche collections, please contact the ERIC Clearinghouse for Junior Colleges, 8118 Math-Sciences Building, UCLA, Los Angeles, California 90024.

References

Bers, T. H. "The Promise and Reality of Women in Community Colleges." Paper presented at the conference of the American Educational Research Association to the Special Interest Group on Women in Education, Tempe, Arizona, November 3-5, 1983. 38 pp. (ED 242 365)

Bragg, A. K. *Fall 1979 Transfer Study. Report 2: First Year Persistence and Achievement.* Springfield: Illinois Community College Board, 1982a. 17 pp. (ED 220 165)

Bragg, A. K. *Fall 1979 Transfer Study. Report 3: Second Year Persistance and Achievement.* Springfield: Illinois Community College Board, 1982b, 20 pp. (ED 230 228)

Bragg, A. K. *Follow-Up Study of Students Transferring from Illinois Two-Year Colleges to Illinois Senior Institutions in Fall 1979. Report 1: Mobility Patterns and Pre-Transfer Characteristics.* Springfield: Illinois Community College Board, 1982c. 16 pp. (ED 220 164)

Cain, R. A. "Equal Educational Opportunity and the Community College." *Journal of Negro Education,* 1982, *51* (1), 16-28.

California Community Colleges. *Transfer Education: California Community Colleges.* Sacramento: California Community Colleges, Office of the Chancellor, 1984. 110 pp. (ED 250 025).

California State Postsecondary Education Commission. *Reaffirming California's Commitment to Transfer: Recommendations for Aiding Student Transfer from the California Community Colleges to the California State University and the University of California.* Commission Report 85-15. Sacramento: California State Postsecondary Education Commission, 1985. 69 pp. (ED 256 398)

Cohen, A. M. "Counting the Transfer Students." *Junior College Resource Review.* Los Angeles: ERIC Clearinghouse for Junior Colleges, 1979. 6 pp. (ED 172 864)

Cohen, A. M. "Hispanic Students and Transfer in the Community College." Paper presented at the Hispanic Roundtable Talk of the American Association of Community and Junior Colleges, Phoenix, Arizona, May 23, 1984. 17 pp. (ED 243 543)

Cohen, A. M., Brawer, F. B., and Bensimon, E. *Transfer Education in American Community Colleges.* Los Angeles: Center for the Study of Community Colleges, 1985. 313 pp. (ED 255 250)

Community College of Philadelphia. *Transfer Outcomes, Fall 1982.* Institutional Report #26. Philadelphia, Pa.: Community College of Philadelphia, 1982. 59 pp. (ED 256 385)

Community College of Philadelphia. *Facts About Former CCP Student Achievement at Transfer Schools.* Institutional Research Report #30. Philadelphia, Pa.: Community College of Philadelphia, 1984. 38 pp. (ED 256 388)

Compton Community College. *Compton Community College's Transfer Opportunities Program: Narrative Report to the Ford Foundation.* Compton, Calif.: Compton Community College, 1984. 26 pp. (ED 258 610)

Davis, E., George, H., and Klauk, E. J. *1984 Graudates of Sinclair Community College: What They Came For, What They Achieved, and What They Thought of Us.* Dayton, Ohio: Sinclair Community College, 1985. 26 pp. (ED 261 741)

Doucette, D. S., and Teeter, D. J. "Student Mobility Among the Public Community Colleges and Universities in the State of Kansas." Paper presented at the Annual Forum of the Association for Institutional Research, Portland, Oregon, April 28-May 1, 1985. 42 pp. (ED 262 844)

Douglas, D., Garcia, M. I., Hernandez, F. M., Locci, S., Long, E., Mendez-Negrete, J., and Ponce, F. Q. *Career Planning for Chicano/Latino Students.* San Jose, Calif.: San Jose City College, 1982. 435 pp. (ED 222 692)

Dunn, R. L., and Greb, J. T., Jr. *Miami-Date Community College Urban Transfer Opportunity Program: Ford Foundation Grant Report.* Miami, Fla.: Miami-Dade Community College, North Campus, 1984. 25 pp. (ED 257 499)

Dzierlenga, D. "Sources of Information: Women In the Community College." In J. S. Eaton (Ed.), *Women In Community Colleges.* New Directions for Community Colleges, no. 34. San Francisco: Jossey-Bass, 1981.

Fernandez, T. V., Raab, M. K., and Smith, B. *Academic Performance of Community College Transferees.* Garden City, N.Y.: Nassau Community College, 1984. 8 pp. (ED 252 268)

Florida State Department of Education. *A Longitudinal Study Comparing University Native and Community College Transfer Students in the State University System of Florida.* Tallahassee: Division of Community Colleges, Florida State Department of Education, 1983. 226 pp. (ED 256 405)

Fonseca, H. R. *Los Angeles Mission College Year-End Narrative Report. Ford Foundation Urban Community College Transfer Opportunities Program.* San Fernando, Calif.: Los Angeles Mission College, 1984. 25 pp. (ED 258 612)

Friedlander, J. *Follow-Up Survey of Students Who Received a Degree or Certificate from Napa Valley College in the 1983-1984 Academic Year.* Napa, Calif.: Napa Valley College, 1985. 9 pp. (ED 256 429)

Garza, M. J. "Current Staffing Patterns." In *Hispanic Achievement: A Commitment of Community Colleges and Business Enterprise. Proceedings of the Hispanic Roundtable Meeting (Phoenix, Arizona, May 23-24, 1984).* Washington, D.C.: American Association of Community and Junior Colleges, 1984. 50 pp. (ED 258 667)

Harris, M. L., and Rohfeld, R. W. *SAT/ACT Preparation Program: A Team Approach.* NCCSCE Working Paper Series, National Council on Community Services and Continuing Education, 1983. 13 pp. (ED 234 861)

Hayward, G. *Preparation and Participation of Hispanic and Black Students: A Special Report.* Sacramento: Office of the Chancellor, California Community Colleges, 1985. 10 pp. (ED 254 285)

Heinselman, J. L. *Transfer Index: One Definition.* Wilmington, Calif.: Los Angeles Harbor College, 1985. 14 pp. (ED 257 512)

Herman, E. F., Gifford, G. L., and Weeks, P. "Women in Technology: The Evolution of a Simple Program That Works." Paper presented at the annual meeting of the American Educational Research Association, New Orleans, Louisiana, April 23-27, 1984. 27 pp. (ED 247 964)

Highland Park Community College. *Highland Park Community College's Ford Foundation Urban Transfer Project.* Highland Park, Mich.: Highland Park Community College, 1984. 112 pp. (ED 257 502)

Honolulu Community College. *Ascent: A Ford Foundation Urban Community College Transfer Opportunities Grant Project. Final Report.* Hawaii: Honolulu Community College, 1984. 79 pp. (ED 257 503)

Houston Community College System. *Houston Community College System Minorities Transfer Opportunities Program.* Houston, Tx.: Houston Community College System, 1984. 12 pp. (ED 258 611)

Hyde, W., and Augenblick, J. *Community College Students, Costs and Finances: A Review of Research Literature.* Denver, Colo.: Education Commission of the States, Education Finance Center, 1980. 121 pp. (ED 192 841)

Illinois Community College Board. *Fall 1979 Transfer Study, Report 4: Third and Fourth Year Persistence and Achievement.* Springfield: Illinois Community College Board, 1984. 25 pp. (ED 254 275)

J. Sargeant Reynolds Community College. *J. Sargeant Reynolds Community College Narrative Report: Urban Community College Transfer Opportunities Program.* Richmond, Va.: J. Sargeant Reynolds Community College, 1984. 13 pp. (ED 258 614)

John Tyler Community College. *1984 Graduate Follow-Up Study.* Chester, Va.: John Tyler Community College, 1985. 116 pp. (ED 259 815)

Johnson County Community College. *Perceptions and Characteristics of JCCC/KU Transfer and "Native" Students, Fall 1983.* Overland Park, Ka.: Johnson County Community College; Lawrence: University of Kansas, 1984. 113 pp. (ED 247 988)

Johnson County Community College. *Students Moving From the Community Colleges to the Public Universities in the State of Kansas: An Initial Statewide Study.* Overland Park, Ka.: Johnson County Community College, 1985. 66 pp. (ED 262 846)

Johnson, R. "Strengthening the Student Aid System in the Community Colleges." In M. Kramer (Ed.), *Meeting Student Aid Needs in a Period of Retrenchment.* New Directions for Higher Education, no. 40. San Francisco: Jossey-Bass, 1982.

Katsinas, S. "Hispanic Student and Staffing Patterns in Community Colleges." Paper presented at the Hispanic Roundtable Talk of the American Association of Community and Junior Colleges, Phoenix, Arizona, May 23-24, 1984. 17 pp. (ED 248 904)

McCabe, R. H. *Evaluating a Community College Transfer Program: A Proposal.* Miami, Fla.: Miami-Dade Community College, 1984. 9 pp. (ED 255 245)

McGrath, D. *Transfer Education Program: Community College of Philadelphia. Report to the Ford Foundation Urban Transfer Opportunities Program.* Philadelphia, Pa.: Community College of Philadelphia, 1984. 12 pp. (ED 256 440)

McMaster, A. *Four Years Later: Class of 1980.* Technical report, 86-02. Trenton, N.J.: Mercer County Community College, 1985. 52 pp. (ED 261 751)

McWilliams, K. *Barrier Reduction Program for Women: Final Report.* Lancaster, Tx.: Cedar Valley College, 1982. 29 pp. (ED 227 911)

Nelson, J. E. "Student Aid at the Two-Year College: Who Gets the Money?" *Community and Junior College Journal,* 1976, *47* (2), 12-13, 15, 17.

Nelson, S. C. *Community Colleges and Their Share of Student Financial Assistance.* Washington, D.C.: College Entrance Examination Board, 1980, 70 pp. (ED 188 718)

Nienkamp, R. L. *1982-83 Graduate Follow-Up Study.* Forest Park, Mo.: Saint Louis Community College at Forest Park, 1984. 113 pp. (ED 247 962)

Olivas, M. A. *The Dilemma of Access: Minorities in Two-Year Colleges.* Washington, D.C.: Howard University Press, 1979.

Orfield, G., Mitzel, H., Austin, T., Bentley, R., Bice, D., Dwyer, M., Gidlow, L., Herschensohn, J., Hibino, B., Kelly, T., Kuhns, A., Lee, M., Rabinowitz, C., Spoerl, J., Vosnos, A., and Wolf, J. *The Chicago Study of Access and Choice in Higher Education: A Report to the Illinois Senate Committee on Higher Education.* Chicago: University of Chicago, Committee on Public Policy Studies, 1984. 351 pp. (ED 248 929)

Osterkamp, D., and Hullett, P. *Re-Entry Women and Part-Time Students: An Overview with Relevant Statistics.* Bakersfield, Calif.: Bakersfield College, 1983. 9 pp. (ED 246 970)

Peng, S. S. "Impact of Student Financial Aid Programs on the Achievement of Equal Educational Opportunity in Higher Education. ASHE Annual Meeting Paper." Paper presented at the Annual Meeting of the Association for the Study of Higher Education, Washington, D.C., April 1979. 29 pp. (ED 174 190)

Peterson, D. *Los Angeles Harbor College Ford Foundation Transfer Report, 1983-84. Interim Report.* Wilmington, Calif.: Los Angeles Harbor College, 1984. 16 pp. (ED 260 738)

Polowczyk, C. *Bronx Community College Urban Community College Transfer Opportunities Program: Ford Foundation Report.* N.Y.: Bronx Community College, 1984. 43 pp. (ED 260 739)

Rendon, L. I. *Mathematics Education for Hispanic Students in the Border College Consortium.* Laredo, Tx.: Border College Consortium, 1983. 120 pp. (ED 242 451)

Renkiewicz, N. *Moving On: A Pilot Study of Student Transfer—California State University, Sacramento, Los Rios Community College District, University of California, Davis.* Sacramento, Calif.: Los Rios Community College District, 1985. 41 pp. (ED 259 802)

Richardson, R. C., Jr., and Doucette, D. S. *Persistence, Performance, and Degree Achievement of Arizona's Community College Transfers in Arizona's Public Universities.* Tempe: Arizona State University, Department of Higher and Adult Education, 1980. 140 pp. (ED 197 785)

Roueche, J. E. "Egalitarianism in College: Problems and Solutions." In F. Harcleroad and Associates, *Serving Ethnic Minorities*. Topical Paper no. 73. Los Angeles: ERIC Clearinghouse for Junior Colleges, 1981. 66 pp. (ED 203 942)

Roxbury Community College. *Roxbury Community College's Transfer Opportunity Program: Narrative Summary*. Boston, Mass.: Roxbury Community College, 1984. 27 pp. (ED 259 763)

Ruiz, A., Kerr, B., Gomez, D., and Berger, R. *Hostos Community College's Integrated Transfer Program: Report to the Ford Foundation*. Bronx, N.Y.: Hostos Community College, 1984. 13 pp. (ED 259 764)

Russo, J. A. "Community College Student Aid: A Hard Look from Within." *Journal of Student Financial Aid*, 1976, 6 (1), 20-27.

Sacramento City College. *Putting It All Together: A Minority Transition Program*. Sacramento, Calif.: Sacramento City College, 1984. 33 pp. (ED 260 740)

Samuels, F. "Closing the Open Door: The Future of Minorities in Two-Year Institutions." Paper presented at the National Adult Education Conference of the American Association for Adult and Continuing Education, Milwaukee, Wisconsin, November 6-10, 1985. 31 pp. (ED 263 946)

Scott, A. *Placement and Transfer Report, 1985*. Binghamton, N.Y.: Broome Community College, 1985. 139 pp. (ED 263 971)

Shimabukuro, M. *Laney College Transfer Opportunities Program, Sponsored by the Ford Foundation. A Narrative Report, 1983-84*. Oakland, Calif.: Laney College, 1984. 26 pp. (ED 258 613)

Seerley, N., and Webb, D. *Gainesville Junior College Minority Advising Program Report, 1984-85*. Gainesville, Ga.: Gainesville Junior College, 1985. 45 pp. (ED 257 508)

Sotiriou, P. E., and Ireland, J. *Los Angeles City College Urban Transfer Opportunities Program: Narrative Report*. Los Angeles: Los Angeles City College, 1984. 21 pp. (ED 257 501)

Valencia Community College. *The Black Advisory Committe of Valencia Community College. Guidelines*. Orlando, Fla.: Valencia Community College, 1980. 11 pp. (ED 229 059)

Weiler, D., Isu, J. A., Nelson, B., Pratt, R. W., Shoenhair, M., and Stern, D. *A Study of California's Community Colleges*. Vol. 1: *Summary and Conclusions*. Vol. 2: *Findings*. Berkeley, Calif.: Berman, Weiler, Associates, 1985. 230 pp. (ED 258 659)

Weintraub, J. I. *A Follow-Up Study of LaGuardia Community College's 1973-79 Graduates*. Long Island City, N.Y.: LaGuardia Community College, 1984. 19 pp. (ED 256 442)

West Los Angeles College. *West Los Angeles College Transfer Opportunities Program: Report to the Ford Foundation*. Culver City, Calif.: West Los Angeles College, 1984. 15 pp. (ED 257 500)

Wintersteen, B. A. "Evaluation of the Social and Academic Problems of the Returning Woman Student." Independent Study Research Paper, North Shore Community College, 1982. 60 pp. (ED 226 767)

Woodland, C. E., and Goldstein, M. S. *Facilitating Community College Access for Minority Students*. La Plata, Md.: Charles County Community College, 1984. 14 pp. (ED 247 994)

Jim Palmer is assistant director for user services at the ERIC Clearinghouse for Junior Colleges, University of California, Los Angeles.

Index

A

Adams decision, 62
Affirmative Action Executive Order 11246, 62
Alba, R. D., 17, 28, 38, 39, 69
Alvarado, A., 72, 78
American Council on Education, 72, 78
Anderson, K., 17, 28
Arbeiter, S., 54, 60
Arizona, University of, 103
Arizona State University, 103
Aslanian, C. B., 54, 60
Astin, A. Q., 73, 79
Astin, A. W., 14, 16, 17, 19, 28, 31, 39
Astin, H. S., 74, 78, 79
Augenblick, J., 109, 111
Austin, T., 112

B

Bader-Borel, P., 32, 39
Bakersfield College (California), 107
Baron, R. F., 64, 67, 69
Basic Educational Opportunity (Pell) Grants, 62. See also Pell Grants
Bensimon, E., 75, 79, 110
Bentley, R., 112
Berger, R., 113
Bernstein, A., 1, 31, 40
Bers, T. H., 76, 78, 79, 107, 109
Bice, D., 112
Birenbaum, W. M., 1, 3, 12
Bishop, J., 82, 89
Blacks: associate degree completion by, 64; average age of, 4; at California community colleges, 24-25; community college enrollment of, 19; future of, 68-69; increase in college enrollment of, 63
Bourdieu, P., 16, 28
Bowles, S., 13, 28, 71, 79
Bragg, A. K., 103, 109
Brawer, F. B., 14, 19, 23, 28, 33, 39, 51, 54, 60, 104, 110

Breneman, D. W., 18, 28, 42, 51
Brickell, H. M., 54, 60
Brint, S., 15, 22, 28, 30
Broome Community College (New York), 102
Bureau of Labor Statistics, 47, 51
Burgan, J. U., 52
Business: and CCT, 48-49; and vocational education, 41

C

Cain, R. A., 106, 109
California: Chicano students in, 33; declining transfer rates in, 32; financial aid recipients in, 84-87; longitudinal study of students in, 44-46; transfer rates in, 23-25, 103-104
California Community Colleges, 104, 110
California Postsecondary Education Commission, 24, 25, 28, 32, 33, 39
California State Postsecondary Education Commission, 104, 105, 110
California State University, 23, 24, 25, 32, 34, 106
California, University of, 23, 24, 25, 32, 106
Campbell, A., 67, 69
Carlson, N., 82, 89
Cedar Valley College (Texas), 108
Center for the Study of Community Colleges, 23, 28, 36, 37, 39
Chicanos, at California community colleges, 33. See also Hispanics
City College of New York, 61
City University of New York, 39, 72, 73
Civil Rights Act, 62
Cleveland State University, 34
Clark, B., 13, 26, 28, 32, 39
Clark, B. R., 14, 28
Cohen, A. M., 14, 19, 21, 23, 28, 33, 39, 51, 54, 60, 101, 104, 105, 106, 110
Colleges, community. See Community colleges

Colleges, two-year, distinction between community colleges and, 19. *See also* Community colleges
Colleges, urban community, 72-75
Colleges, urban women's, 78
Collins, R., 13, 28, 98, 99
Community College of Philadelphia, 102, 103, 110
Community colleges: changes in student body of, 19; customized contract training at, 48-49; decline of transfer from, 23-25; distinction between two-year colleges and, 19; enrollment growth at, 19, 62, 72; entry role of, 19; "filter" role of, 10-11; founding of, 10; growth in number of, 62; and high technology, 46-48; history of social study of, 13-15; limited minority progress at, 64-68; number of women at, 72; outline of debate over, 91-92; promotion of status of women by, 107-108; research findings on, 15-18; rise of vocational education at, 20-23; social composition of, 16; socioeconomic status and attendance at, 20; traditional functions of, 53
Compton Community College, 105, 110
Computers. *See* High technology; Programmers
Continuing education: and equity, 58; potential for inequity in, 57. *See also* Lifelong learning
Corning Community College, 108
Crain, R. L., 48, 51
Credential Society, The, 13
Credentials, 57
Cremin, L., 71, 79
Customized contract training (CCT), 48-49
Cuyahoga Community College, 34, 107

D

Davis, E., 102, 110
de los Santos, A. G., Jr., 62, 64, 69
Deegan, W. L., 38, 40, 48, 51, 54, 60
Degree, associate: increase in award of, 21; minorities obtaining, 63-64

Degree, bachelor's: and community college attendance, 15, 16-17; peak in awarding of, 21
Demographics: of diversity, 6-7; and education in future, 4
Development, adult, consequences of concept of, 56-57
Doucette, D. S., 103, 110, 112
Dougherty, K., 14, 17, 28
Douglas, D., 107, 110
Drisko, R., 48, 51
Dunn, R. L., 105, 110
Dwyer, M., 112
Dziech, B. W., 78, 79
Dzierlenga, D., 107, 110

E

Education: future requirements for work, 8-10; role of, 71. *See also* Higher education
Eiden, L. J., 47, 48, 51
Einstein, M. E., 52
Ellis, R., 95, 96, 99
Equity: and continuing education, 58; and lifelong learning, 59-60
Ethington, C. A., 40
Executive Order 11375, 62

F

Father, and son's educational plans, 95
Fernandez, T. V., 103, 110
Fey, P. A., 54, 60
Financial aid, 5; background on, 81-84; and continuing education, 55-56; data on California recipients of, 84-87; ERIC literature on, 108-109; independent students and, 84; older students and, 82-84; questions and policy options on, 87-89
Florida, declining transfer rates in, 32
Florida State Department of Education, 103, 110
Fonseca, H. R., 105, 110
Ford Foundation, 72, 73, 76, 105
Freeman, R., 21, 28
Freud, S., 91
Friedlander, J., 23, 28, 34, 40, 102, 111
Fuchs, V., 76, 79

G

G.I. Bill, 5, 62
Gainesville Junior College, 107
Garcia, M. I., 110
Garza, M. J., 105, 111
Gender stereotyping, 75-76
George, H., 110
Gidlow, L., 112
Gifford, G. L., 108, 111
Gillespie, D., 82, 89
Gintis, H., 13, 28, 71, 79
Gittell, M., 1, 71, 73, 79
Gladieux, L., 88, 89, 108
Gleazer, E. J., Jr., 54, 60
Goldstein, M. S., 106, 113
Gomez, D., 113
Grant, W. V., 47, 48, 51
Greb, J. T., Jr., 105, 110
Greenbaum, J., 47, 51
Gross, B., 50, 51
Gross, R., 50, 51
Grubb, N., 14, 20, 28
Grubb, W. N., 20, 29, 46, 47, 51

H

Hacker, A., 72, 79
Halsey, A. H., 30
Hankin, J. N., 54, 60
Hansell, S., 22, 30
Hansen, W. L., 1, 81, 83, 84, 88, 89, 90
Harris, M. L., 107, 111
Hayward, G., 106, 111
Hecker, D. E., 52
Heinselman, J. L., 104, 111
Hemond, M. K., 39
Herman, E. F., 108, 111
Hernandez, F. M., 110
Herschensohn, J., 112
Hibino, B., 112
High schools: and immigrants, 61; lack of minority preparation by, 65
High technology, and vocational education, 46-48
Higher education: commuity colleges as bottom track of, 15, 16; community colleges' role for minority entry to, 19; gap between assumptions and reality in, 8; profile of students of, 7; reasons for limited progress of minorities in, 64-68; social and economic consequences of, 55; women in, 76-78
Higher Education Act of 1968, 5
Higher Education Amendments of 1972, 88
Highland Park Community College, 105, 111
Hispanics: associate degree completion by, 64; average age of, 4; community college enrollment of, 19; future of, 68-69; increase in college enrollment of, 63; increasing number of, on faculty, 105-106. *See also* Chicanos
Honolulu Community College, 105, 111
Houston Community College System, 105, 111
Howe, F., 76-77, 79
Hullett, P., 107, 112
Hyde, W., 109, 111

I

Illinois Community College Board, 103, 111
Immigrants, 4, 33, 61
Income: distribution of national, 67; effect of community college attendance on, 15, 17-18; and vocational education, 42, 43, 45
Indians, American, community college enrollment of, 19
Information, 6
Ireland, J., 105, 113
Isu, J. A., 113

J

J. Sargeant Reynolds Community College, 105, 107, 111
Jencks, C., 17, 29
Jobs, and vocational education, 42, 43
John Tyler Community College, 102, 111
Johnson County Community College, 102, 103, 111
Johnson, R., 108, 111
Jussaud, D., 47, 51

K

Kahl, J., 95, 96, 99
Kansas, University of, 102

Karabel, J., 1, 13, 14, 15, 17, 18, 20, 22, 27, 29, 30, 32, 40, 74, 79
Katsinas, S., 105, 112
Kaufman, B., 40
Kelly, T., 112
Kerr, B., 113
Kintzer, F. C., 32, 40
Klauk, E. J., 110
Knoell, D. M., 31, 40
Kuhns, A., 112

L

Lampman, R. J., 84, 89
Lane, W., 95, 96, 99
Laney College, 25, 105
Lasch, C., 57, 60
Laserson, M., 20, 29
Lavin, D. E., 17, 28, 36, 38, 39, 40, 61, 65, 69
Lee, M., 112
Levin, H. M., 46, 52
Lewis, A., 66, 69
Liberal arts: and future world of work, 8-10; need for redefinition of, 11
Lifelong learning: or lifelong schooling, 57-58; possibilities for equity in, 58; social and economic consequences of, 54-56; and social change, 59-60; as substitute for experience, 57. *See also* Continuing education
Literacy, 4
Locci, S., 110
Lombardi, J., 23, 24, 29, 32, 40
London, H. B., 1, 14, 26, 29, 91, 92-93, 99
Long, E., 110
Los Rios Community College, 102
Lukasiewicz, J. M., 52

M

McCabe, R. H., 104, 112
McCartan, A. M., 25, 29
McGrath, D., 105, 112
McMaster, A., 102, 112
McWilliams, K., 108, 112
Maryland State Board for Community Colleges, 43, 51
Massachusetts, University of, 73
Master Plan for Higher Education, 23

Medsker, L., 31, 40
Melendez, S. E., 63, 64, 66, 67, 68, 69, 70
Men, and high-technology training, 48
Mendez-Negrete, J., 110
Mezirow, J., 59, 60
Minorities: assisting, 105-107; associate degree completion by, 63-64; in California community colleges, 45; community college entry role for, 19; continuing education enrollment of, 55; future of, 68-69; increase in college enrollment of, 63; limited progress of, in higher education, 64-68; population growth of, 4; and urban community colleges, 72-73; and vocational education, 50-51
Mitgang, I., 66, 69
Mitzel, H., 112
Mobility, 7; Karabel's thesis on community colleges and, 14; problems of students seeking upward, 92-93, 97-98
Monk-Turner, E., 17, 29
Mother, and students' aspirations, 95
Murtha, J., 40

N

Nassau Community College (New York), 102
National Center for Educational Statistics, 16, 19, 20, 21, 29
Nelson, B., 113
Nelson, J. E., 108, 112
Nelson, S. C., 42, 51, 109, 112
Nelson, S. E., 18, 28
Neumann, W., 93-94, 99
New York, State University system of (SUNY), 32
Nienkamp, R. L., 102, 112
North Shore Community College, 107-108
Northern Arizona University, 103

O

Occupational status, and community college attendance, 15, 17-18
Okun, M. A., 29
Olivas, M. A., 19, 29, 105, 112

Open admissions: background of, 5; ideal of, 3-5; reality following, 74-75
Open-Door College, The, 13
Orfield, G., 65, 69, 106, 112
Oromaner, M., 14, 29
Osterkamp, D., 107, 112
Overeducation, 50

P

Palmer, J., 1, 101, 113
Parents, and student aspirations, 95-97
Parnell, D., 34, 40, 50, 51
Pascarella, E. T., 39, 40
Pell, C., 88
Pell Grants, 84, 87. *See also* Basic Educational Opportunity (Pell) Grants
Peng, S. S., 108, 112
Perkins Vocational Educational Bill, 77
Peterson, D., 112
Pincus, F. L., 1, 14, 20, 22, 29, 41, 42, 46, 49, 51, 52
Polowczyk, C., 105, 112
Ponce, F. Q., 110
Poverty, 5
Pratt, R. W., 113
Pratzner, F. C., 49, 52
Programmers, future for, 47

R

Raab, M. K., 110
Rabinowitz, C., 112
Ravitch, D., 71, 79
Reality: and assumptions about higher education, 8; and open admissions, 74-75
Reeves, R., 88, 89
Reform, educational, 4, 5
Reinherz, H., 91
Rendon, L. I., 107, 112
Renkiewicz, N., 103, 112
Research: on community colleges, 15-18; Karabel's suggestions for future, 25-26
Richardson, G. T., 39
Richardson, R. C., 36, 37, 40
Richardson, R. C., Jr., 26, 29, 43, 52, 103, 112
Riche, R. W., 46, 52
Riesman, D., 14, 23, 29, 93-94, 99

Risk, E. C., 29
Rohfeld, R. W., 107, 111
Roueche, J. E., 106, 113
Roxbury Community College, 73, 76, 113
Rudolf, F., 26, 29, 71, 79
Ruiz, A., 113
Rumberger, R. W., 21, 29, 46, 52
Russo, J. A., 108, 113

S

Sacramento City College, 34, 105, 113
Samuels, F., 106, 113
San Diego City College, 105, 113
San Jose City College, 107
Schmerback, F. A., 60
Schooling in Capitalist America, 13
Scott, A., 102, 113
Seerley, N., 107, 113
Seidman, E., 37, 40
Shavlik, D., 78, 79
Shearon, R. W., 23, 29
Sheldon, M. S., 44, 52
Shimabukuro, M., 105, 113
Shoenhair, M., 113
Silberstein, R. A., 69
Silvestri, G. T., 46, 52
Sinclair Community College, 102
Smart, J. C., 40
Smith, B., 110
Snyder, M. B., 78, 79
Social stratification, Karabel's thesis on community colleges and, 14
Socioeconomic status, and attendance at community colleges, 20
Sotiriou, P. E., 105, 113
Spivak, B. S., 91
Spoerl, J., 112
Stampen, J. O., 1, 81, 83, 88, 89, 90
Stanford University, 95
Stern, D., 113
Stierlin, H., 91, 95, 96, 99
Students: financial aid and independent, 83, 84; financial aid and older, 82-84; first-generation, 94-99; increase in part-time, 54, 72; lack of traditional, 53; London's social study of, 92-93; receiving financial aid in California, 84-87; role of, in decline of transfer, 33-36; study of successful, 93-94

T

Teeter, D. J., 103, 110
Templin, R. G., 23, 29
Testing, for admissions, 66
Tillery, D., 40, 54, 60
Tinto, V., 16, 29
Touchton, J., 78, 79
Tracking: lifelong learning as, 53-60; vocational education as, 14
Transfer: decline of, 23-25, 32-33; effect of, on income, 43; facilitating, 104-105; Ford Foundation program to encourage, 72; future of, 27; institutional-oriented explanation for decline of, 36-38; of many students, 39; problems in obtaining data on, 101-104; student-centered explanation for decline of, 33-36; study of faculty and student views on, 75
Transformation of the Community College, The, 15

U

Unemployment, and vocational education, 42
Underemployment, 50
Urban Community College Transfer Opportunities Program (UCCTOP), 105, 106-107

V

Valencia Community College, 107, 113
Van Dyke, J., 82, 89
Velez, W., 17, 29
Veysey, L., 26, 29
Vocational education: economic effects of, 42-46; and high technology, 46-48; increasing number of students in, 42; minority enrollment in, 64-65; Pincus's conclusions on, 49-51; rise of, 20-23; as tracking, 14
Vocational Education Amendments, 64
Vocationalism, 15
Vosnos, A., 112

W

Warren, J., 33, 35, 40
Washington, declining transfer rates in, 32
Watkins, B. T., 55, 56, 60
Wattenbarger, J. L., 32, 40
Webb, D., 107, 113
Weber, M., 98, 99
Weeks, P., 108, 111
Weiler, D., 104, 113
Weintraub, J. I., 102, 113
Weis, L., 26, 30
West Los Angeles College, 105, 113
Wilms, W. W., 14, 22, 30, 43, 48, 52
Wilson, R., 1, 61, 63, 64, 66, 67, 68, 69, 70
Wintersteen, B. A., 107, 113
Wolf, J., 112
Women: effects of gender stereotyping on, 75-76; and high-technology training, 48; in higher education, 76-78; number of, at community colleges, 72; promoting social status of, 107-108; and urban community colleges, 73; urban women's colleges for, 78; and vocational education, 42, 43, 45
Womens Technical College, 76
Woodland, C. E., 106, 113
Work, future requirements for, 8-10
Wright, D. A., 35, 40

Z

Zwerling, L. S., 1, 2, 14, 30, 32, 40, 53, 60